God as Father

Unveiling God's Love for Sinners, Outcasts, Legalists and Jerks Through the Prodigal Son

Eitan Bar

Preface

T he transformative teachings of Jesus, as encapsulated in one of His parables specifically, have significantly influenced my outlook on life, my understanding of God, and my ministry. For me, the Parable of the Prodigal Son, Luke 15, stands above all others in its impact. It is more than just a story; it is a life-altering narrative that has deeply challenged and reshaped my perceptions.

Through its rich tapestry of rebellion, repentance, and reconciliation, this parable paints a powerful image of divine love and forgiveness. It showcases God not as an austere, rigid, distant entity but as a loving and merciful Father, patient and ever-ready to welcome back even the most wayward of His children. This understanding of God's character profoundly affected how I now view the God of Israel and helped me foster a deeper, more personal relationship with Him.

Dedication

In heartfelt dedication to all the prodigal sons and self-righteous legalist brothers out there. May God's profound grace and unconditional love fill your hearts!

CONTENTS

'After he had spent everything, there was a severe famine   29
in that whole country, and he began to be in need.'
(verse 14)

'So he went and hired himself out to a citizen of that   34
country, who sent him to his fields to feed pigs. He
longed to fill his stomach with the pods that the pigs
were eating, but no one gave him anything.'
(Verses 15-16)

'When he came to his senses, he said, "How many of my   40
father's hired servants have food to spare, and here I am
starving to death!"'
(Verse 17)

'I will set out and go back to my father and say to him: 45
"Father, I have sinned against heaven and against you. I
am no longer worthy to be called your son; make me like
one of your hired servants."'
(Verse 18-19)

'So he got up and went to his father. But while he was   50
still a long way off, his father saw him and was filled with
compassion for him; he ran to his son, threw his arms
around him and kissed him.'
(verse 20)

'The son said to him, "Father, I have sinned against   56
heaven and against you. I am no longer worthy to be
called your son."'
(verse 21)

'But the father said to his servants, "Quick! Bring the   61
best robe and put it on him. Put a ring on his finger and
sandals on his feet."'
(verse 22)

"Bring the fattened calf and kill it. Let's have a feast and   67
celebrate."
Verse 23

"For this son of mine was dead and is alive again; he was   71
lost and is found." So they began to celebrate.'
(verse 24)

'Meanwhile, the older son was in the field. When he   74
came near the house, he heard music and dancing.'
(verse 25)

'So he called one of the servants and asked him what   77
was going on. "Your brother has come," he replied, "and
your father has killed the fattened calf because he has
him back safe and sound."'
(verse 26-27)

'The older brother became angry and refused to go in.   82
So his father went out and pleaded with him.'
(Verse 28)

'But he answered his father, "Look! All these years I've   89
been slaving for you and never disobeyed your orders.
Yet you never gave me even a young goat so I could
celebrate with my friends."'
(Verse 29)

INTRODUCTION

From the beginning to the end of the Scriptures, we are introduced to a God who embodies the roles of a mother, a spouse, a lover, and even a bridegroom.[1] But above all, that of a father. Without a doubt, the Bible's most robust image of God is that of a father who is the ultimate, most perfect father of all. In today's world, however, the concept of a father figure can elicit diverse connotations. Some people may think of a father who is loving, caring, and present in their lives, providing unconditional love and support. In contrast, others may have experienced a father who is abusive, emotionally distant, or demanding, making them feel like they need to constantly prove their worth and earn their father's love and acceptance.

Throughout the New Testament, Jesus consistently refers to God using the intimate term "Abba," reflecting a significant shift in the perception of the Divine from an aloof entity to a caring, involved parent. This Semitic term "Abba," commonly translated as "Father"

---

1. For example, consider Isaiah 49:15, 54:5, 62:5, 66:13; Matthew 6:9; Luke 13:34; Ephesians 5:25; and Revelation 19:7-8. The common thread in all these passages is the same message conveyed in human language: God doesn't hate us; He loves us!

from Hebrew (and Aramaic), encompasses a depth of intimacy and endearment akin to "Papa." In an unprecedented move, Jesus and his disciples address God as "Abba" approximately 150 times throughout the New Testament, signaling an intimate, personal relationship with the God of Israel. This, in fact, was the central theme of their message and why their gospel was considered "good news."

This practice marked a stark departure from the customs of first-century Judaism, where God was often addressed with formal titles such as "master" or "king," emphasizing His transcendence, power, and majesty. By choosing "Abba" over these, or even the more general "God," Jesus and his disciples underscored the personal, loving, protective, caring, and relational aspects of God. This Father—or Papa—figure connotes love, care, provision, guidance, and relationship, painting a picture of God as intimately involved with His people rather than distant, detached, or resentful.

Recall that before Jesus, Israel had not heard the voice of God for hundreds of years. During that span, the people of Israel grew accustomed to the notion that God was not only distant and detached but also angry and hostile. There was a prevailing belief that humanity was so mired in sin and impurity that God had to remain distant. God wasn't viewed as personal and approachable but rather as an entity one should avoid to prevent accidentally inciting its wrath. Ironically, this perspective persists in significant portions of all modern religions.

God our Abba

Abba can only love and educate His children if he is closely connected with them. This paternal imagery taught by Jesus helps us look at the kingdom of God as a familial unit—with God as the Father and us as His children. This underscores the idea of believers being adopted into God's family, a key theme in Paul's letters, such as Romans 8:15-16:

> "The Spirit you received does not make you slaves, so that you live in fear again; rather, the Spirit you received brought about your adoption to sonship. And by him we cry, "Abba, Father." The Spirit himself testifies with our spirit that we are God's children."

As you can already tell, when contemplating God's love, I am invariably drawn to the parental love ideally bestowed upon children—unconditional, relentless, and unwavering. As our Divine Parent, God cherishes us as His children, His love transcending our achievements or failures and embracing us unconditionally, irrespective of our trials, tribulations, or stupidity. God's love is not merit-based. Like the unwavering love parents hold for their children, God's love remains steadfast, regardless of our flaws and mistakes. It's a testament to an unfathomable Divine love that sees beyond our imperfections and shortcomings, forever holding us in an embrace of boundless grace and compassion.

Through the journey of the Prodigal Son, we can discover our Father in heaven's true nature and character. The Parable of the Prodigal

Son is not just a compelling story; it's a compass that helps us reshape our understanding of God's character. Found in Luke 15, this parable hasn't just influenced me—it has transformed my view of God and the purpose of life. It has brought me closer to the heart of God, made me more conscious of my actions and thought patterns, and deepened my commitment to a life filled with grace, compassion, and forgiveness.

I pray that through this small book, you will find God's love in a new way!

BACKGROUND: THE PARABLE OF THE PRODIGAL SON (LUKE 15:11-32)

THE GOSPEL OF LUKE

The Parable of the Prodigal Son, Luke 15:11-32, rests within the fabric of the Gospel according to Luke, one of the four canonical gospels of the New Testament. This Gospel is traditionally ascribed to Luke, a physician and companion of the Apostle Paul. While the authorship and exact date of composition remain topics of debate, it is generally agreed that the Gospel was written in the late first century. The Gospel of Luke is known for its attention to social justice, Christ's love for the outcasts of society, emphasis on prayer, and focus on the Holy Spirit.

The Gospel of Luke starts with the story of Jesus' birth. From there, Luke portrays Jesus as the hope-bringer for Israel, sharing the message of God's Kingdom, especially concerning society's less fortunate. Then, we have this significant section where Jesus and his disciples embark on a journey to Jerusalem. It's reminiscent of Israel's historical journey from Mount Sinai to the Promised Land. Essentially, Luke is presenting Jesus as a modern-day Moses leading his people and a king in David's vein.

As Jesus sets off, he dispatches a group ahead of him to spread the word and prepare for his arrival. Each stop becomes an opportunity to proclaim the good news of God's Kingdom and to rally more people to the cause. Along the route, Jesus delves into essential teachings about handling our money, addressing conflicts, loving the outcast, and treating the less fortunate among us.

The beauty of it all is that Jesus started forming communities in many towns. These communities embrace a fresh approach to life. Greed transforms into generosity, and lingering resentments turn to forgiveness. And here's the kicker: Everyone is welcome. No one's left out, jerks and sinners included.

Remember, the gospels are a narrative about a Jewish Rabbi living in Jewish Israel, and rabbis usually had a following, some of which became vast and influential movements. These respected rabbis would not associate with sinners. In fact, they were conceived as enemies, much like the Gentiles. One of Luke's standout themes, therefore, is the 'good news for the indigent and marginalized.' This was evident both in Jesus' teachings and also in actions: healing those on the periphery, reaching out to the downtrodden, and embracing those often rejected, like tax collectors and prostitutes. This inclusive group forms the heart of his 1st-century Jewish "Jesus movement."

However, not everyone was on board. The religious elite cast skeptical glances at Jesus, especially when he's associating with those they deem "sinners." This sets up a kind of dynamic where we see contrasting dinner scenes. Jesus' meals symbolize God's inclusive love, a feast to which everyone, especially the marginalized, is invited. In contrast, when he attends the dinners of the religious leaders, he challenges them for their exclusivity and elitism. They struggle to grasp Jesus' message, prompting Jesus to share one of his renowned parables.

In Luke 15:11-32, Jesus tells a parable:

11 There was a man who had two sons. 12 The younger one said to his father, "Father, give me my share of the estate." So he divided his property between them.

13 Not long after that, the younger son got together all he had, set off for a distant country and there squandered his wealth in wild living. 14 After he had spent everything, there was a severe famine in that whole country, and he began to be in need. 15 So he went and hired himself out to a citizen of that country, who sent him to his fields to feed pigs. 16 He longed to fill his stomach with the pods that the pigs were eating, but no one gave him anything.

17 When he came to his senses, he said, "How many of my father's hired servants have food to spare, and here I am starving to death! 18 I will set out and go back to my father and say to him: Father, I have sinned against heaven and against you. 19 I am no longer worthy to be called your son; make me like one of your hired servants." 20 So he got up and went to his father.

But while he was still a long way off, his father saw him and was filled with compassion for him; he ran to his son, threw his arms around him and kissed him.

21 "The son said to him, "Father, I have sinned against heaven and against you. I am no longer worthy to be called your son..."

22 But the father said to his servants, "Quick! Bring the

best robe and put it on him. Put a ring on his finger and sandals on his feet. ***23*** *Bring the fattened calf and kill it. Let's have a feast and celebrate.* ***24*** *For this son of mine was dead and is alive again; he was lost and is found." So they began to celebrate.*

25 *Meanwhile, the older son was in the field. When he came near the house, he heard music and dancing.* ***26*** *So he called one of the servants and asked him what was going on.* ***27*** *"Your brother has come," he replied, "and your father has killed the fattened calf because he has him back safe and sound."*

28 *The older brother became angry and refused to go in. So his father went out and pleaded with him.* ***29*** *But he answered his father, "Look! All these years I've been slaving for you and never disobeyed your orders. Yet you never gave me even a young goat so I could celebrate with my friends.* ***30*** *But when this son of yours who has squandered your property with prostitutes comes home, you kill the fattened calf for him!"*

31 *"My son," the father said, "you are always with me, and everything I have is yours.* ***32*** *But we had to celebrate and be glad, because this brother of yours was dead and is alive again; he was lost and is found."*

Now, let's dive into the parable, verse by verse, and unearth all its richness.

'NOW THE TAX COLLECTORS AND SINNERS WERE
ALL GATHERING AROUND TO HEAR JESUS.
BUT THE PHARISEES AND THE TEACHERS OF
THE LAW MUTTERED, "THIS MAN WELCOMES
SINNERS AND EATS WITH THEM."'

(LUKE 15:1-2)

Recently, while searching for an apartment to lease in Haifa, one of Israel's largest cities located on Mount Carmel, I had a conversation with a Jewish realtor. When he inquired about the neighborhoods I was interested in, I mentioned some areas known to be poorer and with people who were "less sophisticated." He questioned, "Aren't you a philosopher or a doctor? Why on earth would you want to live in such areas?" I responded, "These people do not repel me. In fact, I believe God truly loves them." The puzzled Jewish realtor, who did not expect that kind of an answer, struggled to understand my perspective. His attitude mirrored that of the self-righteous religious individuals who listened to Jesus, unable to fathom why would a respected rabbi associate himself with the outcasts.

The tax collectors and sinners

In Luke 15, we're introduced to two distinct groups that must be understood before fully appreciating the parable. On one side, you had some condescending jerks, who happened all to be religious legalists in positions of power, some of whom were also rabbis. On the other, there were the outcasts, the marginalized sinners, trapped in a cycle of poverty that sometimes forced them into theft or selling their bodies to survive, constantly being judged by religious people. These religious leaders criticized Jesus, a Jewish rabbi like themselves, for his compassion towards these "sinners." In their eyes, Jesus must keep pure by keeping away from them. This not only highlighted the profound differences in their theological views of what God is like but also set the backdrop for the parables of the lost sheep, the lost coin, and the prodigal son. Together, these stories underscore the radical inclusivity of Jesus' ministry and the limitless nature of God's grace.

Understanding the reality of life most sinners live in is crucial. The "cycle of poverty" refers to a self-perpetuating pattern in which individuals or families experience poverty and find it difficult to escape. This cycle is characterized by interconnected factors reinforcing each other, making it challenging for those affected to improve their socioeconomic status. Here's a concise explanation:

1. Limited Resources: The spiral of poverty often begins when individuals or families have limited access to resources like education, healthcare, and economic opportunities.

2. Generational Impact: Poverty can be passed down from generation to generation, as children born into poverty may face

similar challenges and limited opportunities.

3. Inadequate Education: Poverty can lead to inadequate schooling, limiting individuals' skills and earning potential, thereby perpetuating the cycle.

4. Limited Access to Healthcare: Poor families may have limited access to nutritious food, clean water, and healthcare, resulting in health issues that further hinder their ability to escape poverty.

5. Low Income and Financial Struggles: Limited education and health issues can lead to low-paying jobs or unemployment, making it challenging to break free from financial struggles and often forcing the poor to sin to survive.

Breaking the cycle of poverty necessitates external interventions, such as enhancing access to education, healthcare, employment opportunities, and robust social support systems. These efforts tackle systemic inequalities and furnish the resources needed to empower individuals and families to rise above poverty.

Additionally, from a spiritual perspective, these measures aid in liberating people from resorting to criminal activities as a means of survival, making helping the poor a Christian moral duty. Consider this: Salvation earned through good works and moral effort would favor the accomplished and privileged. Yet, salvation by sheer grace is equally available to sinners and outcasts, for it is reserved for those who recognize that God's salvation is not something they can earn to begin with. Likewise, we should care about holiness not because "it's offensive to God" or because it threatens our salvation but because we have genuine compassion for those trapped by the destructiveness of sin.

But more than that, Jesus often spoke of loving the needy, the orphans, and the widows, representing anyone who is less powerful than you. If God, who is more powerful, gave His life for you, what should you do for those lesser than you? You will soon find my answer.

The Pharisees and the teachers of the law

The world of first-century Israel was a complex and stratified society. Jewish society, in particular, was highly structured and bound by religious law. The Pharisees were part of the Jewish elite, known for their rigorous observance of Jewish law and tradition. They were highly respected within their communities and significantly influenced religious matters.

The Pharisees and the teachers of the law, also known as scribes, play a recurring role in the New Testament, especially in the Gospels. They were often portrayed as opponents of Jesus and were depicted as being rigid, legalistic, and sometimes hypocritical. Their character was that of pride and elitism. The Pharisees often considered themselves spiritually superior to the general populace. This is evident in passages like the parable of the Pharisee and the tax collector (Luke 18:9-14), where the Pharisee's prayer is self-righteous, contrasting it with the humble plea of the tax collector.

Throughout the Gospels, the Pharisees challenge Jesus, test Him with tricky questions, plot against Him, and even collaborate with other groups (like the Herodians, who had very different political and religious views) to oppose Him.

Conversely, tax collectors were among the most despised figures in Jewish society. Working for the Roman Empire, they were seen as collaborators with foreign oppressors, often accused of extortion and dishonesty. Sinners, a broad term used for those who failed to follow religious laws, were similarly marginalized within their communities. Thus, the sight of Jesus, a respected rabbi, openly associating with such individuals was a cause of scandal and controversy.

Jesus' association with tax collectors and sinners represented a radical departure from the accepted norms of his time. His actions were not simply a matter of social rebellion; they reflected his theological perspective as a respected rabbi, emphasizing compassion, mercy, and grace over strict adherence to religious law. These interactions formed an essential part of his ministry, aimed at societal transformation through the power of love and acceptance.

Jesus' conduct directly challenged the fundamental religious worldview, which believed that God hates sinners and that no righteous person, let alone a rabbi, should associate with them. The religious understanding of God's relationship with humanity was grounded in law and ritual purity. They held that righteousness was achieved through scrupulous adherence to the law, a viewpoint that naturally excluded those who failed to meet these rigorous standards. In their eyes, Jesus' open acceptance of sinners was not merely unorthodox but potentially heretical.

This confrontation between Jesus and the Pharisees provides a valuable insight into the nature of Jesus' mission on earth. The Pharisees' mutterings, "This man welcomes sinners and eats with them," implicitly question Jesus' authority and moral standing. Yet, in a striking paradox, their criticism encapsulates the very essence of Jesus' gospel: God's grace and love are not confined to the righteous but extend to all, especially those marginalized and ostracized by society.

In Judaism, the act of eating with someone is not a trivial matter. It was a statement and represented a significant social and religious act, signifying mutual acceptance and fellowship. By eating with tax collectors and sinners, Jesus affirmed their worth and dignity. His actions challenged the prevailing social and religious norms, advocating a radically inclusive vision of God's kingdom.

These two short verses not only give context to the parables but also underscore the central message of the Gospel of Luke – God's boundless love and mercy for all people. It sets the stage for the subsequent parables in Luke 15, all of which underscore God's relentless pursuit of those considered lost, highlighting that no one is beyond the reach of God's grace. This key confrontation further emphasizes Luke's thematic focus on societal outcasts. The Gospel of Luke is known for its unique emphasis on those on the margins of society - women, the poor, the sick, and the sinners. In that ancient society, if you were poor or sick, you were likely to be more sinful than others, having to figure out less ethical ways to survive in a cruel world. Jesus' interaction with tax collectors and sinners is not an isolated incident but a consistent theme throughout this Gospel, reflecting Jesus' mission: "The Spirit of the Lord is on me, because he has anointed me to proclaim good news to the **poor**. He has sent me to proclaim freedom for the **prisoners** and recovery of sight for the **blind**, to set the **oppressed** free." (Luke 4:18-19).

Jesus' interactions with these marginalized groups were not just about social inclusion but were also deeply spiritual. He was not merely challenging societal norms; he was redefining religious ones. He was declaring a new understanding of righteousness that was rooted in love, mercy, compassion, and grace, not solely in the strict adherence to the law. This perspective significantly deviated from the religious interpretation of the law, which emphasized purity and rejection-separation from sinners to maintain a state of holiness. The fundamentalist-puritan religious leaders in Jesus' day probably viewed him as a liberal, progressive wacko who was compromising God's standards, and they believed his actions proved it (John 8:7; Luke 7:36-50; Luke 19:1-10). They were not evil; they were simply wrong and led by mixed motives, much like the older brother in Jesus' parable.

Jesus' actions, therefore, were not just revolutionary but transformative. They were a radical affirmation of God's love and grace for all of humanity, regardless of societal status, past mistakes, or religious pedigree. His message was an invitation to a new way of thinking and believing, a call to embrace a new understanding of righteousness that was grounded in love, compassion, and grace rather than legalistic purity. The scandal caused by Jesus' association with sinners and tax collectors ultimately points to the broader tension within the Gospel narratives between Jesus and the religious authorities. This tension exposes the divergent understandings of God's nature and how humanity can relate to God. Jesus' actions and teachings consistently challenged the established religious norms of his day, offering a radical reinterpretation of the Jewish faith, one that was more inclusive, compassionate, and grace-filled.

Luke 15:1-2 serves as a reminder of the transformative power of divine love and acceptance. Jesus' radical inclusivity reflected his understanding of God's nature as a loving parent who welcomes all, particularly those who are lost, marginalized, and ostracized. His consistent association with societal outcasts underscores the revolutionary nature of his message and his mission: to establish a kingdom grounded in love, grace, and social justice. A kingdom that includes the oppressed and outcasts of society.

With that context in mind, let's jump into the parable!

'THERE WAS A MAN WHO HAD TWO SONS.'

(VERSE 11)

This seemingly simple statement sets the stage for one of the most profound narratives in the New Testament, offering deep insights into first-century Jewish culture and the broader socio-religious context of Jesus' ministry. In its brevity, the verse encapsulates the intricate familial structure that was common during that era. The nuclear family, with a patriarchal figure at the helm and children, particularly sons, formed the foundation of social and economic life in ancient Jewish society. Patriarchal authority was deeply rooted and widely respected, with the father serving as the head of the family, provider, and figure of authority. The fact that no daughters are mentioned doesn't necessarily mean there weren't any, but they had no legal standing or inheritance rights in the cultural context of the time. Thus, their absence from the narrative may reflect societal norms rather than their actual absence from the family.

In addition, the number of sons mentioned in the verse carries significant meaning. In many biblical narratives, the presence of two sons often symbolizes completeness or balance. This theme can be seen in the stories of Isaac and Ishmael, Jacob and Esau, Moses and Aaron, and others. However, the mention of two sons also hints at the potential for conflict, rivalry, and asking for comparison, as evidenced in those same biblical accounts. Within the context of Jewish inheritance laws, the older son typically received a double portion, which could potentially sow discord between siblings.

Furthermore, this introductory verse foreshadows the unfolding narrative by immediately establishing that the man in the story had two sons. This prepares the audience for a story that involves both sons and potentially explores their differing attitudes and behaviors. It creates a sense of expectancy and anticipation as the audience wonders how each son will interact with their father and with each other.

The cultural and historical backdrop of the verse enhances its significance. Landownership and inheritance held immense importance in the agrarian society of first-century Israel. Land was typically passed down from father to son, with the eldest son receiving a double portion according to the laws outlined in Deuteronomy 21:17. This practice secured the family's economic stability and social status for generations to come. Therefore, the mention of "two sons" would alert a Jewish audience to potential inheritance issues, especially when considering the Prodigal Son's request later in the parable.

Moreover, the two sons become symbolic figures representing the two groups of people listening to Jesus: the sinners and the religious leaders. The father, metaphorically, of course, represents God. This symbolic framework is established from the very beginning, with the audience consciously or subconsciously assigning roles to the characters based on their understanding of Jewish familial dynamics and their knowledge of Jesus' teaching style.

The original audience likely understood the father in the parable to represent God, with the two sons symbolizing Israel's religious people (the older brother) and the nonreligious transgressors (the younger son). If this interpretation holds, we can categorize humanity into two groups: the "older brothers" and the "younger sons." The older brother embodies religious individuals who consider themselves near to God due to their strict adherence to laws and rules. Yet, they might also harbor pride and disdain for those who fall short of their benchmarks. In contrast, the younger son represents the non-religious, secularists, and societal outcasts. The sinners. They might feel alienated by the religious community and, by extension, perceive God as angry, condescending, and vindictive, which could exacerbate their estrangement from faith.

'THE YOUNGER ONE SAID TO HIS FATHER, 'FATHER, GIVE ME MY SHARE OF THE ESTATE.' SO HE DIVIDED HIS PROPERTY BETWEEN THEM.'

(VERSE 12)

The parable opens with an emotionally charged moment set within the social and religious context of first-century Jewish Israel.

In a patriarchal society where respect for elders, especially parents, was paramount, the younger son's request was not just unconventional but outright disrespectful. The distribution of inheritance typically occurred after the death of the father, implying that the younger son did not care much about his father, perhaps even wishing him dead.

The request of the younger son to receive his inheritance prematurely was a shocking deviation from the cultural norms of the time. The land was very much part of the family's identity and the father's stand in the community. This request, in essence, rejected the authority and life of his father, equivalent to expressing a wish for his father's death. The son wanted the father's stuff, not the father himself. The emotional implications of such a request are profound. The younger son appears to be driven by a desire for independence and material wealth and is willing to sever familial ties and societal norms to achieve his goals. His impatience and disregard for his father's feelings reflect a self-centered perspective, revealing a heart consumed by selfish ambition and lack of care. He also seemed indifferent to his family's future, selling a portion of the family's land. Typically, a family wouldn't sell land unless left with no choice.

Put yourself in the father's shoes. What do we usually do when somebody rejects our love and kindness in such a way? We get offended, we get mad, and we get upset. But look at the father's response. Dividing his estate between his sons is equally shocking. The word used for "estate" (βίος) also means "life," "manner of life," and "means of subsistence."[1] The estate is what supports the family's life.

The father acquiesces instead of chastising the son or dismissing his audacious demand. According to the law, the father should have punished the son, and if he decided to put him to death (Leviticus 20:9), no one would object. Yet, he did not take such an action. Furthermore, he neither threatened nor tried to manipulate his son into staying by saying, "How could you do this to me and your mother?"

The emotional toll of this decision is not explicitly stated but can be deeply felt. The father's heart must have been grieved by the younger son's disrespectful demand and the reality of symbolically 'dying' to his sons. Yet, he responds not with anger or retaliation but with a sacrificial love that respects the son's free will. Can it be that the young son never understood his father's love for him and only saw his father as someone who owed him something? How many of us are also like

---

1. John Nolland, Luke 9:21–18:34, vol. 35B, Word Biblical Commentary (Dallas: Word, Incorporated, 1993), 782.

that: Enjoying God's good things but wanting nothing to do with Him?

The emotional dynamics in this verse are mirrored in our understanding of God. The younger son's attitude mirrors our own when we prioritize our desires above loving God and others, essentially wishing God out of our lives to pursue our own ambitions. In contrast, the father's response reflects God's willingness to allow us the freedom to choose our path, even if it leads to pain and loss, respecting our free will. Interestingly, the older son neither rejected the inheritance nor asked his father to delay giving it to him; he gladly accepted his larger portion, just as the younger son received his.

Most pagan nations rejected the concept of free will, believing everything is predestined.[2] However, free will is a foundational concept deeply ingrained in both the Hebrew Scriptures and Judaism. From the very beginning, the Hebrew scriptures emphasize the importance of human agency and the ability to make choices. The narrative of Adam and Eve in the Garden of Eden exemplifies this, as they were free to choose between obeying God's command or succumbing to temptation. Throughout the Hebrew scriptures, individuals are presented with choices, and their decisions carry significant consequences. Judaism upholds the belief that every person possesses free will, granting them the ability to shape their own destiny and determine their moral and ethical actions. Through free will, individuals can actively participate in their relationship with God, make choices that align with divine principles, and fulfill their purpose in this world. It is through the exercise of free will that individuals make mistakes

---

2. Further elaboration in my book, 'The "Gospel" of Divine Abuse.'

and learn through them. Similarly, we see it portrayed here as the father does not assert his authority but allows his child's request to be granted.

But this verse also has implications for our understanding of God's grace. The father's decision to divide his property reveals a love that is not contingent on the son's respect or obedience. Nor does it seem that the father's pride was hurt, as some may expect. This mirrors God's unconditional love for humanity, a grace not dependent on our worthiness or good behavior. It's a grace that respects our freedom, patiently endures our failings, and waits for our return.

Moreover, the father's response challenges the transactional view of God's relationship with people, a view prevalent among religious people of all kinds. Despite the younger son's disrespect and self-centeredness, the father neither punishes him nor denies his request. This counters the legalistic belief that disobedience warrants severe punishment. Instead, it paints a picture of a God who responds to our mistakes with unexpected generosity and patience. While the notion of impressing God with our good deeds is a human-made religious concept, God does allow us to face the consequences of our poor decisions, as about to be evident to the prodigal son.

'NOT LONG AFTER THAT, THE YOUNGER SON GOT TOGETHER ALL HE HAD, SET OFF FOR A DISTANT COUNTRY AND THERE SQUANDERED HIS WEALTH IN WILD LIVING.'

(VERSE 13)

The verse starts with the words, "Not long after that," highlighting the younger son's impatience and impulsiveness. He was eager to strike out on his own shortly after selling his portion of the land, which provided him with his newfound wealth. Clearly, he wished to distance himself as much as possible and pursue his desires. The Greek word συνάγειν ("to gather together") means converting an inheritance into cash. The son sold part of his father's land.[1]

Typically, we flee farthest from situations or places that have caused us pain. This might subtly suggest that the son's actions weren't driven by selfishness alone; perhaps he was also escaping shame or bad treatment by others. From the last part of the parable, it's evident that the older brother held significant resentment towards his younger sibling. Leaving his village wasn't enough; he traveled to a distant country, into

---

1. John Nolland, Luke 9:21–18:34, vol. 35B, Word Biblical Commentary (Dallas: Word, Incorporated, 1993), 783.

exile. For Jews, "distant countries" usually meant exile or other kinds of bad news.

In addition, in the context of the two groups Jesus spoke to, the religious group ostracizes and marginalizes the other group of so-called sinners. Therefore, it's reasonable to assume that in the parable, the older brother, who represents the religious group, may have played a significant role in the younger son's decision to leave home.

Although the text doesn't explicitly state why the younger son desperately wanted to escape, one could speculate. Perhaps he never felt like he could reach the standards set by his older brother. Perhaps the younger son had the soul of an artist who couldn't seem to fit in, or maybe he felt overshadowed by his older brother's devotion, and their fragile relationship played a role. Was the younger son immature and foolish? Quite possibly. However, we shouldn't presume that the younger son's actions stemmed from malevolence or an evil heart. Life is rarely ever in black and white; relationships are invariably intricate and complex, especially within families. I, too, have older brothers, so I am speaking from experience.

The decision to travel to a "distant country" speaks volumes about the younger son's emotional state. It implies a desire to break free from the constraints of his familial and societal roles and to explore life beyond the familiar. It also suggests a deconstruction of his cultural and religious roots, as Gentile lands were often associated with practices contrary to Jewish laws. Also, in Judaism, children are responsible for caring for their aging parents. This wasn't on the son's mind; worse, he felt he wasn't at all needed or wanted.

The emotional journey of the younger son is further highlighted by his indulgence in "wild living." The original Greek term used conveys reckless, extravagant, and self-indulgent behavior. His actions suggest a desire to exercise his newfound freedom to the fullest, even if it means leading an irresponsible and dissolute life. The thrill of independence, coupled with the lure of worldly pleasure, seems to overshadow any consideration of the potential consequences. Obviously, something was wrong with the family dynamics and the upbringing of the younger son that influenced his thinking and behavior. The father's household itself was flawed, much like the fallen creation and the people in it. At some point, something had gone wrong, affecting everything and every family, the prodigal son included. As we will see later, this can only be fixed with love.

However, if love is truly rooted in free will, God's love means He cannot magically fix everything without destroying our free will. Similarly, the father had to allow his sons to act out of their free will. From the father's perspective, the younger son's departure must have been a moment of deep sadness and concern. Although the text doesn't delve into the father's emotions at this point, one can infer a sense of loss and worry. Yet, his earlier decision to grant the son's request implies an understanding of his son's need to carve out his own path, reflecting a love that respects personal freedom, even when it might lead to self-harm.

This verse also carries significant implications for our view of God. The father's response to the son's departure reflects God's respect for our free will. Despite knowing the potential pitfalls, God allows us the freedom to make our own choices, even those that sometimes lead us away from Him. Perhaps it is only when we fall into the deepest of pits that we learn how deep God's love is willing to reach to fetch us out, encouraging us to do the same with those around us who fell into a dark pit.

This truth reflects a God who is not a control freak or coercive but rather invites and patiently waits. The father knows his son will only come to understand his love for him through the upcoming journey and experiences. This holds true in our lives as well. Sometimes, we only come to learn and appreciate what we have lost when we experience the pain of a broken relationship. And what can best fix a broken relationship, if not forgiveness? The young son is about to embark on a dark journey that will ultimately bring him much closer to his father, closer than his "righteous" older brother ever was.

Furthermore, the extravagant and reckless lifestyle of the younger son reflects humanity's propensity to squander God's gifts in pursuit of temporary pleasures. His actions vividly show how we often misuse our freedom, resources, and opportunities, leading to spiritual bankruptcy. This verse profoundly explores human motivations, emotional journeys, and divine love. It captures the audacious break from societal norms and familial bonds by the younger son, his exhilaration of uninhibited freedom, and his subsequent descent into reckless living. Simultaneously, it offers a glimpse into the father's silent suffering, respect for personal freedom, and boundless love. The younger son's actions are a cautionary tale about the perils of unchecked freedom and materialistic indulgence. At the same time, the father's response reveals the nature of God as one who respects our free will, endures our failings, and patiently waits for our return.

The verse also introduces the theme of 'lostness,' which is prominently featured in this parable and the two preceding ones in Luke 15 – the parables of the Lost Sheep and the Lost Coin. In each story, something valuable is lost, diligently searched for, and joyously celebrated upon being found. The younger son's journey to a distant country symbolizes humanity's spiritual quest for meaning in life. Through this journey, we come to learn about ourselves and God. The story begins with one son's departure and ends with another son's departure when the first one returns.

Interestingly, this verse also sets the stage for the exploration of the older brother's character, whose self-righteousness and legalistic attitude are challenged by the father's unconditional love and forgiveness for the wayward younger son. Although the older brother is not explicitly mentioned in this verse, his silent presence serves as a counterpoint to the younger son's reckless behavior. He, in contrast to his younger brother, doesn't shame the father and leaves the family behind. Deep inside, perhaps the older brother is happy, believing he now has his father's undivided attention. Maybe he scorned his little brother and enticed some family members against him. One can only speculate. However, little does he know that just as a shepherd leaves the flock to find the one lost sheep, his father's attention will be focused outside the house, sitting on the balcony and eagerly awaiting the return of his other son.

'AFTER HE HAD SPENT EVERYTHING, THERE WAS A SEVERE FAMINE IN THAT WHOLE COUNTRY, AND HE BEGAN TO BE IN NEED.'

(VERSE 14)

F rom the outset, the verse emphasizes the son's wastefulness: "After he had spent everything." The Greek word used here suggests lavish, extravagant spending that leaves nothing. The younger son, who demanded his share of the inheritance not so long ago, now finds himself penniless. His reckless spending and uncontrolled living have led him to a state of destitution. But clearly, he was seeking something. Something to rest his hurting soul.

In a predominantly agrarian society where wealth was tied to land and livestock, a person's survival was closely linked to their resources. The son didn't use his money to invest or buy property, but in wastefulness, lost everything. Therefore, he would have been seen not just as foolish but mainly as endangering his very survival. There was no welfare; he was now at the mercy of the pagans, who historically were not friendly to the Jews. His actions would have also been frowned upon by his Jewish contemporaries, who valued frugality, saving for the future, and wise management of resources.

In addition to his own wastefulness, external circumstances – "a severe famine in that whole country" – further exacerbate the son's situation. To the Jewish listener, famine reminded biblical stories. For instance, in the days of Abraham and Sarah, a severe famine led them to Egypt.

Schadenfreude, the pleasure derived from seeing others in suffering or in trouble, is a combination of the German nouns *Schaden*, meaning "damage" or "harm," and *Freude*, meaning "joy." Getting to know several "Pharisees" and how they think in my own life, I'm convinced the Pharisees listening to Christ were gloating in their hearts. This is because the story arrives at a turning point, introducing a drastic change in the younger son's circumstances that offers profound insights into human vulnerability, divine providence, and the nature of God.

However, we know that God uses all life circumstances, including hardship and distress, to bring the best of outcomes.

By now, it's probably been months, if not years, since he left his home. Famine was common in the ancient Near East, especially in Israel and the south of it, and it often resulted from inadequate rainfall. It could lead to devastating economic and social conditions, especially for someone without resources or familial support.

The son's transition from wealth to need would have been a harsh reality check. The poor are usually more accustomed to survival mode, unlike someone like the young son who grew up pampered by his wealthy family. The emotional toll of this change cannot be understated. He likely experienced fear, regret, and desperation as he confronted the consequences of his actions. Perhaps now he understands that he had it all but never knew how to appreciate it.

The text says, "he began to be in need," suggesting a newfound recognition of his dependence and vulnerability. This need was both material and transcendental – a deep yearning for the security and belonging he once took for granted. But I'm sure he also felt it in his quickly shrinking, hungry belly.

The news of a severe famine that had reached the whole country likely reached his father. From the father's perspective, we can only imagine the worry and concern he might have felt for his son. Perhaps at this point, knowing his son's character and the reality of the famine, the father assumed it was only a matter of time before his lost son would return. Despite his son's disrespectful departure, there was zero schadenfreude in the father's heart. His love for his son has remained, probably leading to anxiety about his son's well-being in a distant land hit by severe famine.

Famine has profound implications for our comprehension of God. The Jews might interpret the younger son's predicament as mirroring the promises of the Law. At the conclusion of the Law, God warns Israel that if they stray from Him, He won't protect them, leaving them vulnerable. This manner of expressing God's wrath is evident in the Old Testament, and the Jewish audience likely drew parallels between that and the younger son's plight.

Despite the son's failings, the verse subtly hints at the nature of God's grace. The severe famine, while causing suffering, also serves as a catalyst for the son's self-realization and repentance. This aligns with the biblical theme of God using trials and hardships to draw us back to Him. The verse portrays the dire consequences of the younger son's reckless decisions and the harsh realities of his new circumstances. It explores the emotional journey of the young man who, having squandered his resources, now finds himself in a state of desperate need.

It invites us to consider the probable emotions of the distant father, anticipating his worry and concern for his son's well-being despite the physical and relational distance between them.

This portrayal also illuminates profound truths about the nature of God. It showcases a God who allows us to face the consequences of our actions yet uses these very situations to draw us back to Him. This is the God of the Bible – patient, just, and full of mercy. The younger son's situation serves as a metaphor for our spiritual condition when we distance ourselves from God, emphasizing our inherent need for divine grace.

Furthermore, the famine serves as a poignant symbol of the spiritual barrenness that results from turning away from God's presence and provisions. The son's state of need, both material and spiritual, underscores the insufficiency of worldly pleasures and the futility of seeking satisfaction apart from God.

Simultaneously, the son's desperate situation sets the stage for a profound demonstration of divine grace in the latter part of the parable. By allowing the son to reach a point of utter need, the narrative prepares us for the lavish grace of the father, who welcomes his lost son back with open arms. This stark contrast underscores the Christian understanding of grace as God's unmerited favor towards us, regardless of our unworthiness.

Thus, this verse offers a stark yet hopeful picture of the human condition and God's response to our failings. Through the younger son's dire circumstances and the father's anticipated concern, we are invited to reflect on our own spiritual journeys, our need for divine grace, and the ability to be encouraged by the boundless love of a God who waits patiently for our return, and the return of all others, no matter how badly we or they have messed things up. The verse also serves as a sobering reminder of our choices' destructive potential while holding out the promise of divine grace and redemption. It offers a profound exploration of the human-divine relationship within the Christian faith, inspiring us to seek God's grace and mercy in our own relationships.

'SO HE WENT AND HIRED HIMSELF OUT TO A
CITIZEN OF THAT COUNTRY, WHO SENT HIM TO
HIS FIELDS TO FEED PIGS. HE LONGED TO
FILL HIS STOMACH WITH THE PODS THAT THE
PIGS WERE EATING, BUT NO ONE GAVE HIM
ANYTHING.'

(VERSES 15-16)

We arrive at an impactful and emotionally charged moment in the narrative of the Prodigal Son. The younger son's action speaks volumes about his dire circumstances, and this verse gives us invaluable insights into the societal norms of the time and the internal turmoil of the characters involved.

Historically, the younger son's act of hiring himself out is an acute representation of his desperate state. The Greek term 'KOLLAO,' which means 'to glue' or 'to join oneself,' suggests that the younger son was not merely looking for employment, but he was at such a desperate point that he was willing to attach himself to anyone who could provide for his basic needs, much like slaves.

Jewish culture during the first century in Israel was hierarchical, with a clear societal structure. Being a hired hand, especially for a Jew in a foreign land, would have been viewed as a significant degradation in status. The younger son, who was once a part of his father's household, has now been reduced not only to the status of a hired hand, humiliating in itself, but of a Jew who hires himself to gentiles, underscoring the extremity of his fall. Since Jews despised Gentiles and had strict regulations regarding interactions with them, working directly under them would have been seen as the ultimate degradation. Not only was the younger son isolated from his familial and community ties, but he also found himself in a position that was antithetical to Jewish cultural and religious norms.

This degradation is further highlighted when we consider that the younger son was sent to feed pigs – animals deemed unclean by Jewish Law and symbolizes deception. Leviticus 11:7 reads, "And the pig... is unclean for you." For a Jew, not only consuming pork but even touching a pig was unthinkable. So, the act of serving gentiles and their pigs would have been the ultimate humiliation, further emphasizing the gravity of the son's predicament.

Understanding the depths to which the younger son has sunk, we can infer his feelings of desperation, shame, and perhaps regret. He likely felt a profound sense of loss, not just of his material wealth but also his social standing, his dignity, and the comfortable life he once knew. His previous demand for freedom and autonomy has led him to a state of complete dependence and servitude, revealing a stark contrast between his previous pride and current humiliation.

Although the father does not appear in this verse, we can imagine the anguish and concern he may have felt if he knew about his son's condition. As a loving father, his heart would have been heavy with worry, knowing the severity of the hardship his son was enduring.

Interpreting this verse through a theological lens provides valuable insights into our view of God. The younger son's act of hiring himself out and his new job of feeding pigs illustrates the spiritual state we may find ourselves in when we choose to live independently of God. It's not that God hates or punishes us, but that we suffer the consequences of our decisions. The son's predicament mirrors our own when we stray from God only to find ourselves spiritually starved and degraded.

If my son chooses to go to a risky town at night against my advice, he might get hurt not because I've punished him for disobeying me but because I'm not there to protect him. Similarly, we should not equate the younger son's suffering with God's anger. The consequences he faces result from the absence of protection that comes from distancing himself from his father. In Old Testament terms, Israel understood this absence of protection as the 'wrath of God.'

Throughout the Hebrew Scriptures, God is portrayed as allowing freedom of choice, even when those choices lead to our downfall. This highlights God's respect for human agency, a key facet of His character. But this verse also sets the stage for God's grace – though we may turn away from Him and face harsh consequences, God is always ready to welcome us back, just as it will soon be demonstrated by the father in the story.

Luke 15:15 starkly portrays the younger son's desperation and humiliation. We see the depths of the son's degradation through a historical and cultural lens. We feel the characters' emotions and potential motives – the son's desperation and the father's worry. We also gain insights into the character of God – a God who respects human freedom, even when it leads to self-destruction, yet remains loving, patient, and ready to welcome us back with open arms. Still, it also sets the stage for a powerful revelation of divine grace, a plot twist Jesus' audience is unprepared for.

The son's act of hiring himself out to feed pigs symbolizes what often happens when we seek our own good alone in selfish ways: We exchange true freedom for servitude, integrity for degradation, and abundance for scarcity. Just as the younger son exchanged his birthright and a life of comfort for fleeting pleasures and eventual destitution, we too often trade the eternal riches offered by God for transient and ultimately unsatisfying worldly pursuits.

On another level, this verse subtly illuminates the shortcomings of the world and its false promises. The citizen of the foreign country, who might initially have appeared as a redeeming figure to the desperate son, fails to provide adequate care and meets the son's needs grudgingly, if at all. This highlights the stark difference between the world's treatment of the son and the father's loving and generous nature, which we will see in later verses.

Looking at it through this lens, this verse brings to the fore the stark contrast between the world's inability to satisfy our deepest needs and God's extravagant grace and provision. While the world offers pig pods, God prepares a feast; while the world bestows servitude, God extends sonship.

Meanwhile, the father remains a poignant presence, though physically absent in this verse. His love and concern for his son can be inferred, mirroring the loving concern that God continually has for us, even when we walk away from Him. Contemplating his lost son, the pain and anxiety he must have felt mirrors God's sorrow over every lost soul struggling to figure life out.

If the audience thought the son already hit the lowest point of his life, they had a surprise coming. The "pods" in this context are most likely carob pods, a common food for pigs in our Mediterranean region. These pods were edible but hard, mostly tasteless, and lacked substantial nutritional value, essentially a sustenance of last resort for the desperate and needy because they were cheap and available. But considering the severe famine, that was probably the default of many.

Again, remember the cultural context. Pigs were considered unclean animals in Jewish society. Hence, the younger son's willingness to share pig food amplifies the depth of his desperation and degradation. The younger son's desire to consume pig fodder underscores the depth of his hunger and his fall from grace. This is perhaps a situation only Jews could genuinely appreciate.

The son is likely grappling with extreme desperation and profound regret at this juncture. He must be contrasting his dire circumstances with his earlier life, one filled with privilege and comfort. His hunger extends beyond the physical; it's also a deep emotional and spiritual craving for the life he once knew—a life he probably now views as unattainable. This stark disparity between his past and present, between abundance and want, prosperity and penury, belonging and estrangement, would undoubtedly provoke a deep sense of remorse and a yearning to go back home. It wouldn't be unreasonable to assume that thoughts of ending his life may have also crossed his mind.

The phrase "but no one gave him anything" illustrates the stark reality of the world's indifference. The world can "be there for you" when it gets something from you. However, once you fall, everyone seems to disappear. This might be a critique of the world's lack of compassion and grace towards sinners and those in need.

In regards to Jesus' audience, the religious figures likely felt a surge of pride, gloating, and a sense of superiority, while the sinners likely assumed they were being criticized. "Great," they might have thought, "yet another rabbi telling us we're unworthy lowlifes in God's eyes." However, as with any compelling story, the audience was in for a treat.

'WHEN HE CAME TO HIS SENSES, HE SAID, "HOW MANY OF MY FATHER'S HIRED SERVANTS HAVE FOOD TO SPARE, AND HERE I AM STARVING TO DEATH!"'

(VERSE 17)

Ever since our encounter with the Tree of Knowledge, we've been driven by a curiosity for new experiences, often pondering, "I wonder what that would feel like?" This quest is relentless and can form a relentless cycle. Yet, God likely deemed this experiential journey crucial for imparting us with essential insights about Him as we walk in this journey. We can only genuinely grasp something when it resonates emotionally with us. Thus, the answer isn't to diminish or belittle human emotions and feelings; after all, they are God-given gifts to us.

So, when we read that "he came to his senses," it becomes clear that his experiences illuminated insights he previously lacked. He felt a myriad of emotions, such as sorrow, loss, regret, and desperation, which propelled him toward a newfound understanding and spurred him to alter his path. In the son's case, it has not yet happened. The main feeling he is experiencing at the moment is that of hunger.

In the historical context of first-century Israel, servants and hired workers were a common feature of well-to-do households. These individuals had a secure livelihood and were provided for by their masters. They did not need to eat pig's food and even had food to spare. The son's comparison of his situation to that of his father's hired servants further emphasizes the magnitude of his predicament. Even these hired workers, lower in social status than he was as a son, had more than enough food while he was on the brink of starvation. And while they enjoyed the company of each other, he enjoyed the company of...swine.

Verse 17 marks the turning point in the narrative, where the younger son recognizes his predicament and yearns for change. In fact, he is realizing he is about to die of starvation. The son wasn't motivated by the realization that he had offended and wronged his father; he was driven by hunger. The son's wish to return home and his acknowledgment of his father's kindness toward the servants underscore the father's good-hearted nature. His reference to his father's hired servants suggests a sense of humility and an acknowledgment of his dreadful situation. This awakening is crucial for his transformation and eventual return to his father.

Although the father is not physically present in this verse, one can infer his character from the son's reflection. Despite the son's initial lack of respect for his father, he recognizes his father's fair treatment of his servants, which reflects his compassionate nature and generosity—virtues that the son now fully recognizes. Often, we only appreciate people's positive characteristics once in retrospect. This memory of his father's kindness stirs a deep longing in the son's heart, not necessarily for his father, but for his father's generosity.

This verse profoundly impacts our understanding of God. The

younger son's return to his senses is symbolic of our own moments of spiritual awakening. When we are entangled in the pursuit of worldly pleasures, we often neglect our spiritual health. But in moments of great crisis, we are called to reflect on our choices and their consequences, just like the younger son. This verse portrays God as a patient and loving Father who gives us the freedom to make our own choices but is always there to welcome us back into His grace.

The verse also carries theological implications concerning repentance. Some doctrines romanticize repentance, associating it with salvation, but the fact is that this wasn't so much a change of heart as it was a change of stomach. The son doesn't want to starve to death. Clearly, his journey home wasn't motivated by a desire to mend his fractured relationship with his father. Rather, he intended to repair that relationship as a means to an end: to eat and survive. There was nothing about reuniting with his father for the sake of their lost bond or to mend his sins; he was driven by the prospect of improving his dire living conditions. In his own words, "At home, even the hired servants have enough food to spare, and here I am, dying of hunger!" His driving force was not genuine reconciliation; it was survival. This can't be labeled as true repentance.

What propelled him to leave in the first place was the same illusion that was driving him back: the belief that things are better elsewhere. The son was not contemplating the emotional pain or disappointment he had inflicted on his father or his family. He remained self-centered, focused solely on his own needs and survival. Pay attention to what the Scripture omits. It doesn't say, "He felt remorse." It doesn't say, "He regretted the pain he had caused his father and family." Instead, the Scripture says, "When he came to his senses." In other words, only when he began to think rationally and logically did he recognize the disparity between who he had become and who he could have been and how he could utilize that realization to survive.

Before this moment, before he betrayed his father, abandoned his family, and squandered his inheritance, name, and reputation, his thinking was flawed, and consequently, his life followed a destructive path. It's crucial to understand that the root of our problems often lies in our mindset. Thus, the solution to our problems must also be transforming our thinking. A shift in perspective can be the first step towards a meaningful change in one's life circumstances.

This reminds me of King David. After committing adultery and murdering Uriah, David also did not repent but hid his actions for about a year until God finally sent Nathan to deliver the bad news—his sanctions. Society usually sanctions you, but no one but God can threaten you when you are the king. Only after hearing what was about to happen did David repent. His repentance, genuine or not, was fear-driven and in an attempt to ease the penalty. In a sense, David was coerced into repenting, which alleviated the sanctions. However, I don't believe David's salvation was ever at stake. If it had been, surely Nathan would have said something about it.

Likewise, the father's love for his younger son was never questioned. However, much like David, the younger son suffered because of his decisions. The son's realization, regret, and decision to return home can't be seen as a genuine act of repentance, but he undoubtedly reached a point, fearing his imminent death, that finally drove him to change his ways. We see the son finally acknowledge his mistakes and consciously decide to change his course, turn away from destructive paths, and choose better ways.

The son's comparison of his condition to his father's servants shows his desperation and his newfound humility and self-awareness. This humility is often the first step toward reconciliation, forgiveness, and true repentance. It symbolizes our own spiritual journeys, wherein acknowledging our sins, feeling regret, and deciding to change are integral to our spiritual walk and quality of life.

In summary, Luke 15:17 underscores the power of self-reflection. The verse presents a moment of self-realization for the prodigal son, marking a turning point in his life once he realizes he has reached a dead end. This encourages us to introspect, to evaluate our choices, and to learn from our mistakes.

'I WILL SET OUT AND GO BACK TO MY FATHER
AND SAY TO HIM: "FATHER, I HAVE SINNED
AGAINST HEAVEN AND AGAINST YOU. I AM NO
LONGER WORTHY TO BE CALLED YOUR SON; MAKE
ME LIKE ONE OF YOUR HIRED SERVANTS."'

(VERSE 18–19)

In Jewish culture, phrases like "I am no longer worthy" and "I have sinned against heaven and against you" became phrases that carry significant weight. The phrase, "I am no longer worthy," is also used by Jacob (Genesis 32:10) when returning home from exile. Jacob was also the younger son. The younger son's motives in Jesus' parable are complex and layered when contemplating his return home. His prepared apology is an official, diplomatic utterance rather than a personal, emotional confession. The son's use of this phrase implies that he recognized his actions as more than just a slight against his father; he saw them as a breach of divine law. Alternatively, it could be what he thought his father wanted or needed to hear to allow him to become a servant. Was the son slowly becoming genuinely repentant on his way back home, or was he calculatingly manipulating his father's emotions to achieve his own ends? Hard to say...

The sincerity of the son's prepared apology remains a point of conjecture. He acknowledges his sinful and rebellious behavior, suggesting he either genuinely believes he's no longer worthy of his father's love or anticipates his father will shun him after his actions. Unfortunately, this notion—that accumulating sin causes God to hate us and minimizes his love for us—still prevails in religious teachings today.

The son plans to ask his father if he can return as a mere servant, hoping to someday make amends by paying back his debt. Much like the prodigal son, many people today feel they are unworthy of God's love. Recently, I stumbled upon a widely-followed reformed YouTube channel (close to 100 million views) featuring popular Calvinist pastor Tim Conway, who, in one of his sermon preachings, asserted:

> "What Scripture tells us is that all of mankind are children of wrath. We are objects of the hatred of God by nature. We don't deserve His love... God is not unjust to hate mankind because mankind is a hateful thing by nature. It ought to be hated!"[1]

However, this misguided belief of the son (and Pastor Conway) is incompatible with the father's belief. As events would later demonstrate, his father believed just the opposite: no matter his son's actions, he would always be deserving of his love.

The emotional landscape of the son in the narrative is complex. Does he still feel negative feelings toward his family? Or is he start-

---

1. Tim Conway, "God Hates the Sin and the Sinner", YouTube, Sep 18, 2018.

ing to feel sorry? Perhaps it's a mosaic of feelings and motivations. He is seemingly willing to do whatever it takes to survive, even if it means sacrificing his own pride. A multitude of feelings—fear, hope, shame—must be swirling within him, but what dominates is an overpowering need for reconciliation and forgiveness, seeking sustenance, which drove him to make his journey back to his father. What moves the son is not the feeling of "I am sorry" but the feeling of "I need help." The son's motivation, however, wasn't relevant for the father.

Understanding the cultural nuances of this verse enriches its meaning, particularly in the context of Jewish culture, where familial ties and responsibilities are highly revered. The son concludes that if his father allows him anywhere near his estate, he will plead to be received as a lowly hired servant, content to earn his keep and perhaps, eventually, repay some of it to his father. Hired servants, in this culture, held a markedly lower social status. While some were almost like family, provided with room and board, others, like hired servants, were day laborers with less intimate connections to the household, having to travel back and forth daily. The son's willingness to settle for this lowly position illustrates his desperation. Imagine how degrading and humiliating it would be for him to work as a hired servant for his family.

The son's internal deliberations and subsequent choice to return provide an opportunity for us to reflect on our own life journeys. Even if our motives are far from pure, the acknowledgment of our errors is the first crucial step toward transformation. It also urges us to reconsider our understanding of sin, not just as a violation of divine law but as transgressions against other people. This perspective emphasizes the need to seek forgiveness not only from God but also from those we've harmed. After all, it's not God who suffers from our wrongdoings; it's our fellow humans. So, even if our motivations are flawed, as they were for the younger son, a heartfelt apology can mend dead relationships.

Moreover, when the son admits, "I am no longer worthy to be called your son," he acknowledges not only that he has squandered his material inheritance but that he has grievously breached the trust and honor bestowed upon him by his father. To fully grasp the gravity of this verse, it's essential to comprehend the societal norms of ancient Jewish culture. Sons were more than mere family members; they were heirs and perpetuators of the family lineage. The son's departure, especially after demanding his inheritance, was a serious affront to these cultural values.

This narrative, rich with emotional and cultural nuances, serves as an allegory for our relationship with God. The son's sentiments of unworthiness mirror the feelings of many who find themselves distant from God due to their life choices. The son's willingness to be considered "like one of your hired servants" highlights the depth of his despair. In his eyes, he has fallen so far from grace that he no longer deems himself deserving of familial love or status. This, again, is a common view among religious people today, believing they are unworthy of God's love despite the fact we are all His children (Acts 17:29; 2 Corinthians 6:18). The belief we are unworthy of God's love due to our transgressions is a recurrent theme in many religions.[2]

However, as the son soon discovers, his father's love always remains steadfast and unchanging. This will be a reminder to us as well that as God never changes, so His love for us never changes. Like some of us, the son underestimated his father's capacity for grace, presuming he might not even be allowed to serve as a mere hired hand. Many people, including devout Christians, similarly underestimate the depth of God's grace and love. They pray for minimal mercies, like sparing their lives by allowing them servitude, unaware of the boundless love that God actually offers.

In conclusion, the son, plagued by guilt and desperation, never truly understood his father's heart. He mistook the nature of his father's grace, assuming it to be limited and conditional. The tragedy lies in the son's misinterpretation of his father's love, a lesson that prompts us to consider whether we, too, misunderstand the vastness of God's love and grace for us.[3]

---

3. For an extended discussion on love, refer to my book "Holy Love: A Modern-Day Definition."

'SO HE GOT UP AND WENT TO HIS FATHER.
BUT WHILE HE WAS STILL A LONG WAY OFF,
HIS FATHER SAW HIM AND WAS FILLED WITH
COMPASSION FOR HIM; HE RAN TO HIS SON,
THREW HIS ARMS AROUND HIM AND KISSED HIM.'

(VERSE 20)

The son is making his way home and his father spots him, not when the son is steps away from the estate but while he is still a significant distance off. Remarkably, it wasn't a servant who noticed the returning figure and informed the father; the father himself saw. I can imagine in my mind how the father would rise every morning at 4:45 a.m., prepare meals, and journey for an hour to the closest mountain. After reaching the summit, he would position himself for the best possible view. Perhaps he even set up camp there, resolved not to descend until his son's return. Numerous possibilities clouded the father's thoughts: had his son perished, or had he found a different life elsewhere? Yet, the father's unwavering gaze betrayed his hope. Deep within, he believed his son would come back.

Another aspect to ponder is that the father ran to meet him upon spotting his son, not vice versa. An often overlooked detail is the substantial distance the two must have covered together, conversing privately. Did the son share tales of his misadventures? Did the father express how profoundly he'd missed him and update him on family affairs during his absence? Such moments are left to our imagination.

Nonetheless, the father's actions speak volumes. His unwavering gaze, constantly searching the distance, signifies an undying hope, an endless watch. Picture the father at the boundaries of his land each day, eyes relentlessly scanning the horizon, heart oscillating between hope and despair. His vigilant stance wasn't merely physical but also emotional and spiritual, a testament to a love that transcends both time and circumstance.

This vigilance starkly contrasts with the image that religious legalists of the day would have likely conceived. Many in Jesus's audience, grounded in a stringent legalistic interpretation of Jewish law, may have predicted a narrative where the father's righteous indignation trumps his paternal affection. *"Ah,"* they might think, *"the father wants to see the son from afar so he can stone him to death without anyone even knowing."* Some in Jesus' audience likely expected to hear something like: *"But when he was still a long way off, the servants told the father, who was filled with much fury. Taken by his wrath and 'holy hatred,' the father refused to hear his son, flogged and bruised him for his wicked sins, and cast him into a pit in anger!"*

But that is not the story Jesus tells. Instead, the father sees, runs, embraces, and kisses his returning son—radical acts that flip the cultural and religious norms. This scenario should ring a bell for Jews. In Genesis 33, it is Esau who runs out to meet his prodigal brother Jacob, who came back from a distant land and "threw his arms around his neck and kissed him" (Genesis 33:4). In this way, Jesus criticizes the religious leaders (represented by the older brother); instead of the older brother running to greet his brother and bandage his wounds, it is the father who takes the initiative, acting alone. Remember, Esau was the father of Edom, Israel's sworn enemy. It was Esau who showed love and compassion to Jacob. But here, the self-righteous older brother wants nothing to do with his sinful brother.

What happened next is even more overwhelming. Before there was any apology, without any word of repentance by the son, the father ran to him, hugged and kissed him! He did not act like a father but like a mother.

The son is undoubtedly weighed down by shame and fear upon his return. As he approaches home, he might anticipate various reactions: anger, disappointment, or even indifference. Yet, he couldn't have anticipated the sight of his father, the patriarch, running towards him like a small child, disregarding societal norms.

But here's what the younger son didn't know for a very long minute: Was his father running at him in anger, intending to punish him, or in excitement, eager to embrace him? Imagine the confusion and fear on the son's face as he saw his father charging toward him, uncertain whether to stand his ground or flee for his life.

To fully appreciate the father's actions, we must understand them within the framework of first-century Jewish society. This was a culture where honor was everything, particularly for elders and, most especially, for patriarchal figures. Elders would traditionally wait to be approached, not the other way around. Running was a child's act, inappropriate for an adult, and unthinkable for an elderly man of stature. However, this father defies all such social codes and etiquettes. The act of running itself was laden with profound meaning—a visual proclamation that his love for his son outweighed his concern for societal norms or personal dignity. It was as though he was saying, "To hell with decorum; my child is home!!"

The next act was even more ground-breaking when the father reached his son: he hugged and kissed him! Notice this was before any apology was offered and before any words of remorse were spoken. Again, the kiss came before any confession was offered. The father received this boy before he ever said a word. He embraced the son while he was still dressed in his filthy rags. He didn't say, "You smell like a pig! Go clean up, and later, we'll talk." He embraced him; he kissed him. The kiss came before any confession was offered. This must have implications for our theology as well.

This was an embrace and kiss of preemptive grace, a physical manifestation of an emotional and spiritual truth. The father's arms wrapped around the son, and his lips met his face in intimacy as tangible tokens of immediate forgiveness and unconditional love. The son must have been enveloped not just in his father's arms but also in a sense of sheer astonishment and relief. The act of the father's embrace and kiss symbolizes more than just a reunion; it's a theologically rich statement akin to the Christian tenets of salvation and grace. In Middle Eastern culture, a man kissing another man is not sexual but a strong cultural expression of love and acceptance, akin perhaps to the holy kiss mentioned in the Epistles.

At this juncture, it is crucial to recognize that the father had every religious and legal right to condemn his son. In fact, Deuteronomy prescribes stoning for a rebellious son. However, the father's grace was counter-cultural and counter-legalistic. His grace has overcome the law. It was anathema to the conventional wisdom of the day, an almost scandalous act of benevolence that would have likely left Jesus's audience in a state of cognitive dissonance.

And what about the father's feelings? He was undoubtedly awash with a complex blend of relief, joy, compassion, and love. Here is a point often ignored: The father was not excited because his son repented but because he realized he was still alive!

There's no veneer of guardedness or reserve in his demeanor; his emotions are on full display, almost recklessly so. This is not the modulated affection of a parent who follows the strict societal honor and shame ledger. This is the unbridled love of a father who values relationship over rules, who celebrates life over punishment, and whose heart beats to the rhythm of grace, not legalism. There is absolutely nothing in this verse about repentance. That, whether it was genuine or not, is yet to come at this point.

It's important to note that the story addresses some deeply ingrained theological misconceptions, particularly the notion that divine love has to be earned or can be forfeited through human sinfulness. The son's worth, his father affirms, is inherent, not earned! If you must earn your father's love, it's not true love. His value is immutable, rooted not in what he has done but in who he is—a beloved child. And remember, the prodigal son represented the sinners and outcasts.

Basically, Jesus says God doesn't wait for sinners to repent before He loves them. He just does. They are just as much His beloved children as any other condescending jerk out there who thinks they are better than others. This perspective starkly contrasts the transactional view of God held by many, where love is a reward for good behavior, and repentance is the 'admission fee' for divine forgiveness.

In closing, Luke 15:20 serves not merely as a plot point in a parable but as a spiritual lodestar. It challenges and upends societal and religious assumptions about justice, honor, and love. Jesus articulates a theology of extravagant grace, preemptive love, and radical inclusivity through it.

'THE SON SAID TO HIM, "FATHER, I HAVE
SINNED AGAINST HEAVEN AND AGAINST YOU. I
AM NO LONGER WORTHY TO BE CALLED YOUR
SON."'

(VERSE 21)

T he son is the first to speak—a copy-paste from his carefully prepared speech. One gets the sense that he has likely committed it
to memory during his long journey back home. But it's crucial to note
that even when armed with rehearsed words, apologizing becomes
significantly easier when one already knows forgiveness was assured.
His confession is designed to address two distinct but intertwined
spheres of his transgressions: the heavenly and the earthly. In this
context, "heaven" serves as a metaphor for the Divine. By first admit-
ting his wrongdoings against heaven, the son demonstrates a nuanced
understanding of the spiritual and ethical laws he has contravened.
This is not merely a case of financial recklessness or youthful folly; it's
an acknowledgment of violating divine mandates that govern morality
and righteousness.

Subsequently, the son articulates his failures towards his father,
thereby acknowledging the earthly repercussions of his actions. This
bifurcated confession is an acute reminder that we lose points in heav-

en when we hurt those on earth. Interestingly, the son knew that he had already been forgiven even before uttering his apology. His father's demonstrative embrace and kiss weren't mere gestures but substantive embodiments of unconditional love and grace. It's an emotional elixir that amplifies remorse while simultaneously alleviating the burden of shame, granting the son a space for confession and authentic reconciliation.

Can you imagine the psychological shift that occurs when you realize you're forgiven even before your apology leaves your lips? The emotional texture of this moment for the prodigal son is rich with feelings of profound remorse, humility, and vulnerability. In a society where honor carries immense value, declaring oneself "unworthy" is tantamount to self-abasement of the highest order. The overwhelming warmth of his father's unconditional acceptance likely magnifies the son's feelings of unworthiness.

It's essential to understand that the son isn't merely seeking forgiveness; he's forgoing all claims to his family status, placing himself wholly at the mercy of a father whose forgiveness he believes he's already secured. Translated into theology, God doesn't wait for your repentance to forgive. He simply forgives. However, it's upon you to recognize and accept that you're forgiven. If you truly accept this forgiveness, then it will manifest in recognizing yourself as a child of God and living as one. No child of God should be burdened by shame and guilt. Beyond forgiving oneself, it's vital to harness this truth to extend forgiveness to others.

The father, for his part, must have had an emotional maelstrom raging within him as he listened to his son's confession. The son's admission of guilt would likely validate the father's own deep hurt while simultaneously piercing his paternal heart. No good and loving parent wants to see their child brought low, suffused with guilt, especially when that guilt could easily have been avoided. Yet, here is also a moment that underscores the father's wisdom in receiving his son back into the fold. He sees his son's humility as confirmation that his extravagant grace was not misplaced. His decision to forgive isn't merely validated; it's vindicated. This love doesn't just welcome back; it fully restores, without reservation or condition, offering a homecoming that erases past sins and sets the stage for a renewed relationship.

This narrative mirrors our relationship with God in many profound ways. The prodigal son represents everyone who has strayed from the divine path, seeking pleasures and freedoms but in all the wrong places, only to realize the spiritual bankruptcy of a life without any divine guidance. The moment of confession, where the son acknowledges his sins against heaven and his father, parallels individuals' confessions, acknowledging their failures before God, asking to once again receive protection and guidance.

The idea that our sins are not only violations of divine edicts but also have ramifications in our earthly relationships is a powerful one. It reinforces the interconnectedness of the divine and the earthly, urging individuals to see the broader implications of their actions. However, our repentance pertains to the quality of our relationship with God, not our salvation. No loving parent will ever kill his child if they fail to repent, and God is more loving than any human parent. We are forgiven simply because God is love. You may disagree, but I don't believe you will lose your salvation just because you failed to repent for another stupid thing you did. God isn't some petulant kid with a short fuse; He's a loving father. However, His forgiveness doesn't negate the fact He will also allow you to experience the consequences of your actions, for better or for worse.

This is symbolized by something most Christians today are unaware of, yet all of Jesus's followers, as native Hebrew speakers back then, would have understood intrinsically. The very name of Christ reveals God's forgiveness. His name wasn't "Jesus," but "Yeshua." YESHUA translates to "The Lord is Salvation." For Jews, salvation isn't a reaction to human behavior but an intrinsic attribute of the God of Israel, who is "mighty to save" (Zephaniah 3:17). We must not only recognize but apply it; God can't think or do for us.[1]

The son's self-declared unworthiness is ultimately proven false. He is indeed worthy of his father's love, not because of what he has or hasn't done, but simply because he is his son. Likewise, God's forgiving nature is a constant; He always forgives. And yet, He expects us to adjust our ways of thinking and acting in accordance with His loving nature.

The father was not particularly concerned about hearing his son's prepared apology in its entirety. This is evident when he interrupts the son before he can even complete his rehearsed speech. One could speculate that the father discerned the speech as more of a formal

---

1. The "faith vs. works" argument regarding salvation in Christianity is foreign to the Jewish people, whereby you earn God's favor through deeds and works, but not His salvation. Judaism teaches and believes that "All of the Jewish people, even sinners and those who are liable to be executed with a court-imposed death penalty, have a share in the World-to-Come." (Mishnah Sanhedrin 10:1).

gesture than a genuine expression of remorse. The fact that the father cuts off the apology might signify that his love and grace are so overflowing that they don't require a formal confession as a precondition for acceptance.

Could it be that the father's interruption was a subtle way of saying, "Your words, however heartfelt or diplomatic they may be, are not the currency that buys my forgiveness or love"? It's as if the father is teaching a lesson that transcends the formalities of apologies and enters the realm of pure, unconditional love—a love that doesn't need to hear the right words to validate its existence.

For the father, perhaps the son's return was enough of a gesture, signifying a change of heart. After all, actions often speak louder than words. By merely coming back, the son had already made a significant statement about his desire to make amends and rejoin the family.

This perspective adds another layer to the theological undertones of the narrative. It suggests that divine forgiveness might operate on similar principles: it doesn't require us to always articulate our shortcomings in eloquent apologies; sometimes, our heartfelt desire for change and help from above is enough. Sometimes, in our weakness, "the Spirit himself intercedes for us through wordless groans." (Romans 8:26)

The father is making one thing clear to his son right from the start: grace is not earned through crafted words or deeds but is a gift, generously and freely given (Ephesians 2:8-9).

'BUT THE FATHER SAID TO HIS SERVANTS, "QUICK! BRING THE BEST ROBE AND PUT IT ON HIM. PUT A RING ON HIS FINGER AND SANDALS ON HIS FEET."'

(VERSE 22)

There exists a gap, spanning hours or perhaps days, between the previous verse and now. In this interlude, the son and the father walked side by side, sharing a private space of reconciliation and reconnection. It wasn't just the prodigal son who made his way back to the estate as is commonly perceived. Instead, they both entered the estate together, symbolizing unity, mutual acceptance, and a renewed bond. This collective return is a testament to the idea that true reconciliation is a shared journey where both parties come together in mutual understanding and healing. It underscores the significance of not just the act of return but of communal re-entry into a space of love and acceptance. In other words, when you forgive someone, it's not just by words; it's also by actions- you bring them back into the community.

The father's response mirrors the sentiments found in Paul's iconic chapter on love, 1 Corinthians 13. Not only is the father swift to forgive and forget the past, but he also embodies the virtues mentioned by Paul: patience, without keeping a record of wrongs, rejoicing in the truth, and enduring all things in love. Just as love never fails, the father's love for his son remains unwavering despite the circumstances.

We see no judgment of the son by the father for his sins, no preaching to him what true repentance should look like, and no reminding him of his past mistakes to embarrass him. It's a portrait of redemption, an act of letting go of your own pride in order to restore someone else's honor, and an undeniable testament to unconditional love. The father didn't love and forgave the son because he returned or said the right things. He forgave and loved the son because he was his child.

I believe that if the child chose to leave again and venture into another predicament, his father would once again step outside and search for him, ready to embrace him with love. If Jesus taught us that we ought to forgive endlessly, then the father in His parable surely would too.

Notice that the father doesn't ask his servants to bring a cane and Bible so he can punish him and put a Bible in his hands. In fact, by delving into the historical context, we gain a deeper understanding of each item the father asked to bring his son.

The "**best robe**" belongs, of course, not to one of the servants but to the father and is saved for special events and celebrations. This wasn't just any robe; the word used (στολὴν) means a long robe. The upper classes wore that kind of robe. It was a symbol of honor and status. By requesting this robe for his son, who had just returned after squandering his father's wealth, the father wasn't just covering his physical nakedness; he was reinstating his honor, his place in the family, and erasing the shame that came with his prior actions. This gesture, especially in front of the household servants, is a public proclamation that the son's past is forgotten, and his original status in the family remains unchanged. The father didn't only show compassion by forgiving his past mistakes. He gave grace by reminding his son—and everyone else around—that he is still his loved child.

The father achieves multiple symbolic purposes by putting the best robe on his returning son. First, he restores his son's position in the family, signifying that the son is not a mere servant but holds all the rights and privileges of being a family member. The robe also serves as a clear sign of acceptance, acting as a physical manifestation of the father's unconditional love and forgiveness for his wayward son. This gesture additionally reaffirms the son's identity as a beloved family member, tapping into biblical symbolism where clothing often relates to one's identity.

The robe sets the tone for the following celebratory feast, emphasizing the immense joy surrounding the son's return. Furthermore, the robe stands in sharp contrast to what the son was likely wearing—probably filthy rags—which amplifies the transformative power of his father's acceptance and love. Imagine the prodigal son, swept away by his sins and returned filthy and smelling like pigs, dressed in a glorious robe while entering the family estate. This probably evoked the memory of Isaiah's words in the minds of Jesus' hearers:

> "All of us have become like one who is unclean, and all
> our righteous acts are like filthy rags; we all shrivel up
> like a leaf, and like the wind our sins sweep us away."
>
> Isaiah 64:6

The sins of the son were covered with the father's luxurious robe.

But that's not the first time our heavenly Father has done such a thing. In the Garden of Eden, God also cloaked Adam and Eve with robes, the tunics of skin He had made for them.

The "**ring**" also held significant value. It wasn't just a piece of jewelry. The ring likely was one of the father's signet rings. In ancient times, a signet ring would be used to seal official documents, representing the king's authority and confirming tribal identity. By looking at the ring, you can tell what family the person wearing it belongs to. This ring would have had more than just financial value; it symbolized the father's authority and trust, effectively restoring the son's position in the family. He was reinstating his son fully into the family's operations and decisions. Given that a ring is a circle without a beginning or end, it can also be seen as a symbol of eternity, continuity, and completeness, which parallels the themes of endless love and grace throughout the parable.

Lastly, the "**sandals**." Remember, in his prepared speech, the son had said he was no longer worthy to be called a son and hoped to find work as a hired servant. This might suggest that either the son took off his sandals or had none because they were already worn out, and he couldn't afford to replace or fix them.

In the cultural context of the time, slaves typically went barefoot, whereas free members of the household wore sandals. By giving his son sandals to wear, the father clearly states: "The son is not to be treated as a slave or a servant but as a free person and a full member of the family." This simple act of providing footwear reinstates the son's lost dignity and reaffirms his status within the familial structure.

The sandals also serve a functional role—they protect the feet, enabling travel and interaction with the world. Symbolically, this could represent the son's renewed ability to walk a righteous path, now guided by the wisdom gained from his previous misadventures and the forgiving love of his father. The act of putting sandals on his son's feet can also be seen as a gesture of that father recognizing his son's growth, now being able to lead because he experienced and understands perfectly well what love and grace look like, but also what pain of wrongdoing looks like. That's the dual major degree needed for any true leader.

Thus, the sandals are not just an afterthought; they are integral to the theme of restoration and reconciliation in the parable. They encapsulate the father's desire to fully reintegrate his son into both the family and society, emphasizing dignity, freedom, and care.

Consider the feelings and motives of each character:

The father's actions are filled with profound compassion and urgency. His priority wasn't to lecture or reprimand but to restore and heal. The fact that he did not even let the son finish his prepared speech shows he had no interest in dwelling on the past. His immediate instructions to the servants reflect a heart bursting with joy and a desire to right every wrong, not by words but by actions. This clearly reflects the God of the Christian narrative – a deity not focused on our past mistakes but on our return to Him.

The **father** didn't need to punish him before he could forgive him. Nor did he need to punish someone else to "release his wrath" before granting forgiveness. True forgiveness doesn't require any conditions or exchanges; one absorbs and takes on the burden personally.

The **son**, on the other hand, must have been overwhelmed. After preparing himself for a possible rejection or, at best, a conditional acceptance, he's met with gifts of honor, authority, and identity. These gestures, which came without even hearing a full confession, would have instilled a sense of deep humility, gratitude, and perhaps even disbelief. It encapsulates the sheer magnitude of grace – receiving forgiveness and honor that he did not feel he deserved.

The **servants** play a subtle but important role here. In ancient Jewish culture, the household staff would be keenly aware of family dynamics. They act as silent witnesses to this restoration, and their participation in these acts of grace signifies the entirety of the household, acknowledging the son's return to his original status. Their actions also demonstrate the ripple effect of grace – its impact isn't limited to the individual receiving it but extends to the entire community. If a family, community, church, or nation doesn't show grace, it's only because its members won't. A truly Christian nation lives out grace, even to enemies.[1]

---

1. This was not meant to be a political statement. Of course, allowing your enemy to kill you isn't grace. A nation should also have law and order and be able to protect itself.

"Bring the fattened calf and kill it. Let's have a feast and celebrate."

Verse 23

E ating meat was a rare occasion, let alone eating a calf—and not just any calf, but a fattened one! This was extremely rare and meant that the father was yet again reducing his wealth, but this time, it was for the sake of celebration. If you were disturbed by the younger son's wastefulness, it's clear his father wasn't frugal either.

Fattened calves were especially fattened for special occasions and were reserved for significant festivities such as weddings and holidays. The choice of the calf, as opposed to a lamb or goat, also underscores the magnitude of the celebration. It was meant to feed a very large number of people, indicating that this was not just a family dinner with close friends but a grand feast, possibly involving the entire community. This wasn't just a meal. The father said, "Let's have a feast and celebrate." Music and dancing were involved as well. Much like in weddings!

The mere act of slaughtering the fattened calf reveals a lot about the father's character and emotions. The father's love raises the question: If loving parents are willing to love their children unconditionally despite their imperfections, why would we think our Father in Heaven would love us any differently?

In his state of despair, the prodigal son probably hoped for a bowl of yesterday's leftover falafel and some dry pita bread to go with it. If he's lucky, maybe it will even be heated up. But he was likely very doubtful his father would offer him even a lowly position in his estate. However, the father opts for an elaborate celebration instead of offering a mere morsel or a simple meal. This choice is a testament to his overwhelming joy and relief upon his son's return. If you have ever owned a dog and can remember how excited and thrilled they get when you return home, that's probably how the father felt when his son returned home. The sheer happiness of reuniting with his lost child overshadows any traces of anger or disappointment. This grand gesture communicates that the son's return is not a somber moment but a time of jubilation.

But here's a detail that's often overlooked: Fattening a calf is not a quick process; it can take several months. This suggests that the father had anticipated the son's return and began the preparations well in advance. This further emphasizes why he was outside, waiting and watching with such anticipation.

For the prodigal son, witnessing preparations for such a feast with no less than a fattened calf in his honor might have been overwhelmingly humbling. He had returned home with guilt, expecting perhaps condemnation or, at most, conditional acceptance. However, the father's decision to throw a grand celebration symbolizing complete restoration might have left him with feelings of profound gratitude, unworthiness, and awe. This was more than just about physical sustenance; it was an affirmation of his place in the family, an assurance of unconditional love, and a clear message that his past was forgiven and forgotten.

Unfortunately, this is not always the message preached in Christian churches. People reject Christianity for several reasons, and I have found that two of them stem from the same core reason: Fear. People fear that God will judge, condemn, and punish them and that Christians will do the same. Sadly, some Christians judge, control, and scare people away and paint a frightening picture of God, further alienating individuals.

In the parable's narrative, the wider community and the household also play an indirect role. Hosting a feast requires preparation, and the servants, as well as the community members invited, would share in the joy, partaking in the festivities and rejoicing for the upcoming celebration. This communal celebration symbolizes the collective joy that the return of a lost one brings. It emphasizes that personal joys and sorrows are deeply intertwined with the collective experience in close-knit communities.

The threat of death that overshadowed the prodigal son in this story wasn't because of something the father would do to him if he didn't return. The father kept no torture chamber hidden in some faraway basement where he planned to burn him alive after finally finding him. The son experienced hell simply by being away from his father's house.

Theologically, this verse has profound implications regarding the Christian understanding of God's nature. In this parable, the father symbolizes God, and his actions offer insights into God's character. The father's joy mirrors God's joy in heaven over one child of God willing to come to Him. The grandeur of the feast, represented by the fattened calf, mirrors the joy in heaven of all who are celebrating with the Father. It's as if they all celebrate graduation—a graduation from the school of maturity, learning the true meaning and value of love, sacrifice, grace, and humility. Now, he is finally trained to be a true leader himself.

Moreover, the feast is also an emblem of communion, a sacred act in Christian tradition. It echoes the Last Supper, where Jesus broke bread with His disciples, and the eschatological feast, the great banquet believers look forward to in the heavenly realm. In both contexts, the meal is symbolic of God's fellowship with humanity and His desire to be in intimate communion with His creation.

In conclusion, while seemingly straightforward, this verse is a narrative powerhouse. It encapsulates the cultural norms of the time, portraying a lavish celebration reserved for the most special occasions. The father's decision to hold such a feast underscores the depth of his love, forgiveness, and joy upon his son's return. The prodigal son's probable feelings of awe and gratitude became the moving force for his greatest transforming moment in life. I believe this proves that it is God's grace, not fear, that enables us to grow spiritually.

You, dear reader, are a child of God as well. Quit reminding yourself of every past mistake you have made, quit dwelling on last week's failures, and start dwelling on God's love and grace, especially in the context of how you can mirror that to others.

"For this son of mine was dead and is alive again; he was lost and is found." So they began to celebrate.'

(Verse 24)

In the Old Testament, the theme of being "lost and found" manifests in several profound narratives that symbolize the intricate relationship between God and His people, Israel. The iconic story of the Exodus sees the Israelites "lost" in the bondage of Egyptian slavery, only to be "found" or liberated by God through the leadership of Moses. Similarly, prophetic books like Hosea and Isaiah depict Israel as a wayward wife or child who has strayed from God's path and needs to be "found" again by returning to Him. The story of Jonah adds another layer, showing how one can be "lost" by actively running away from God's will, only to be "found" through extraordinary circumstances. Lastly, the narratives in Ezra and Nehemiah recount how the Israelites were "lost" during the Babylonian exile but were eventually "found" when they returned to Jerusalem, re-establishing their unique covenantal relationship with God. These stories underscore the idea that even when His people are physically or spiritually lost, God remains active in seeking to restore them.

From a cultural perspective, the concept of someone being "dead" and then "alive again" in literature usually wasn't meant literally. In many cultures, particularly within Jewish traditions, declaring someone as "dead" often meant the relationship was dead. For example, you might hear, "Are you still in touch with John?" followed by, "Oh no, that relationship is long dead." Saying someone was "dead" often symbolized being cut off from their life or declaring them an outcast. For instance, if a Jewish person from an ultra-orthodox family were to confess that Jesus is their Messiah, the family would likely consider them "dead" and perform a funeral. In the context of the parable of the prodigal son, the term "dead" signifies that the relationship was lost (much like the coin and sheep). The son had distanced himself from the safety and protection of his home and ventured into a faraway land, both literally and metaphorically. Thus, his return is akin to a resurrection, a transition from "death" to life. The lesson is clear: if even the godly father in Jesus's parable can show such extraordinary compassion and offer unconditional grace to a wayward son, so should we!

The prodigal son, hearing his father's words, probably experienced mixed emotions. Elation at being accepted, relief at being forgiven, and perhaps a touch of shame for his past actions. The acknowledgment from his father, a figure of authority and respect, would've profoundly impacted him. It was validation that he was truly forgiven and accepted back into the fold.

While not directly voiced in this verse but probably included in the celebration, the servants and the community would've been witnesses to this profound moment. Observing the patriarch's open display of emotion would've instilled the event's magnitude in them. By partaking in the ensuing celebration, the community was sharing in the collective joy and relief of the family, emphasizing the interconnectedness of individual joys and sorrows in tight-knit communities.

Theologically, this verse places a significant emphasis on the role of feelings and emotions in our understanding of God, underscoring His nature. Rather than depicting God as emotionless or as an angry, punitive moral monster lying in wait for us to make our first mistake in order to burn us alive, the parable paints a picture of a compassionate, loving, and grace-filled Father. In this narrative, the father figure, who symbolizes God, represents a deity that doesn't just begrudgingly forgive; he genuinely rejoices in the return of those who left Him.

The poignant phrase "was dead and is alive again" is a powerful metaphor for the spiritual journey many undertake. It encapsulates the transformative experience of someone who turns away from a life ensnared by selfishness and experiences a spiritual rebirth. This transformation is of our view of God. A new understanding that God is a Father who loves all His children, no matter how far away they've gone. This perspective offers a richer, more nuanced understanding of God's nature, highlighting that He is not only a moral lawgiver but also a loving parent eager to celebrate grace whenever possible! This gives believers a more complete, compassionate framework for understanding their relationship with God and one another and underscores the boundless capacity for forgiveness and renewal in the Gospel.

Celebrations in ancient Middle Eastern cultures were often elaborate events that could last for several days or even up to a week. The festivities included feasting, singing, dancing, and various ceremonies. For example, in the Book of Judges, Samson's wedding feast lasted seven days (Judges 14:12).

'MEANWHILE, THE OLDER SON WAS IN THE FIELD. WHEN HE CAME NEAR THE HOUSE, HE HEARD MUSIC AND DANCING.'

(VERSE 25)

In a typical Jewish household of that era, the oldest son would be considered the primary heir, inheriting a double portion compared to any other son. He was expected to take on more responsibilities and maintain the family's legacy. He was also the man in charge outside the house, far away in the family field. The field was not just a place of labor but also represented the very sustenance and future of the family. The verse emphasizes his dedication and commitment to his familial responsibilities by mentioning that the older son was in the field.

Now, a Jewish listener hears that the older brother is in the field and remembers that in Genesis 4, Cain, also the older brother, is out in the field where he kills his younger brother, Abel, after realizing God showed him affection. This mirrors the state of the older son's heart in the parable, as he, too, wishes for his younger brother's death.

The older son was out of the house, possibly for several days, taking care of business in the family's faraway field. This becomes evident when he hears the music only upon getting close to the house. But as he approaches the house and hears music and dancing, the ambiance is out of sync with the routine he's familiar with. Musicians? Dancing? These were not daily occurrences on the estate; they were reserved for special occasions like weddings or significant religious festivals. Given that no such event was scheduled, curiosity, surprise, and perhaps even irritation are all easily imagined.

As he draws closer to the house, he would likely feel a mix of emotions: surprise at the unexpected celebration, curiosity about the cause, and perhaps a twinge of resentment or confusion as to why he, the dutiful son, was not informed or included from the start. Given the story's backdrop, it's not hard to imagine him pondering, "After all I've done and sacrificed for the family, why am I being kept in the dark?"

Moreover, if we consider the broader narrative where he later discovers the reason for the celebration, these feelings would likely intensify, adding layers of resentment, jealousy, and a sense of injustice. Why should the wayward sinful son, who squandered his inheritance, be celebrated while he, who remained steadfast, is overlooked?

The servants and other party attendees were very much a part of the celebration. Their participation in this joyous occasion reflects the father's desire to share his happiness with everyone. They could likely sense the moment's significance, even if they might not fully understand the older son's forthcoming feelings of neglect.

From a theological perspective, the older son's character is profoundly relatable. He represents many of us who feel that God should highly value our steadfastness, dedication, rigidity, and good works or those who feel that God's blessings are unevenly distributed despite their faithfulness. Why do some who seemingly stray from the path receive blessings while those who are dutiful feel overlooked?

In the wider scope of the parable, the father's eventual response to the older son provides profound insight into God's nature. But focusing solely on this part of the story, we get a glimpse of God's celebration for every far-from-perfect person wanting to be by His side. The self-righteous never appreciated the fact that sinners are welcomed by the Father just as much as they are, those who didn't squander everything they had. It's a poignant reminder that God's celebratory heart isn't reserved only for those who kept all the rules but also for those who have had a hard time and broke many rules.

While the festive sounds highlight a moment of divine rejoicing, they simultaneously foreshadow a profound human struggle for inclusivity, recognition, and understanding. It's a testament to the intricate layers of human nature, the vastness of God's love, and the sometimes challenging intersection of the two.

'SO HE CALLED ONE OF THE SERVANTS AND
ASKED HIM WHAT WAS GOING ON. "YOUR
BROTHER HAS COME," HE REPLIED, "AND YOUR
FATHER HAS KILLED THE FATTENED CALF
BECAUSE HE HAS HIM BACK SAFE AND SOUND."'

(VERSE 26-27)

The relationship between the oldest son of a wealthy household and his servants was hierarchical. However, in daily life, it was common for members of an extended household, including servants, to be well-acquainted with family affairs, especially in a scenario where a son dramatically left and returned. Many of these servants were not merely hired hands; they lived on the property, worked closely with the family, and shared joys, sorrows, and secrets in the household.

The older son's curiosity is evident. Having heard the unexpected sounds of jubilation, he needed clarity. But underneath that curiosity might be layers of emotions. Was there trepidation? After all, he had not been informed of any significant event. Was there resentment? He might have felt slighted, given that he was apparently the last to know of this significant family event. Rather than rushing into the house, his decision to ask a servant suggests a hesitance, a momentary pause to prepare himself for whatever awaited. It could also indicate a reluctance to confront his father immediately without full knowledge of the situation.

From a broader perspective, the older son's inquiry also hints at a deeper, more universal human sentiment. Many of us, when faced with unfamiliar or unexpected scenarios related to faith and God's actions, have asked a version of the older son's question: "What is going on?" Why are things unfolding in a way that seems contrary to our understanding or expectations of justice, merit, and reward?

The older son's experience mirrors those moments when we see others, whom we deem less deserving, receiving blessings or grace. It's a moment of reckoning where our understanding of justice and grace is challenged. It's not always easy for the legalist within us to accept the fact that God also rains on sinners.

The parable, in its entirety, is a profound lesson on God's boundless and often confounding mercy. However, this specific verse emphasizes the initial human reaction to such mercy — confusion, the need for clarity, and perhaps a hint of indignation. In the broader narrative of the Bible, God's actions and decisions have often been met with human confusion. From Jonah's anger at God's mercy towards Nineveh to Job's friends trying to rationalize his suffering, the Scriptures are filled with moments where God's actions challenge human conceptions of righteousness and justice.

The older son's question underscores the idea that our human understanding is limited. We smell the BBQ, see the party lights shining, and hear the music, so to speak, and yet we often lack the divine perspective to comprehend God's grace fully. The older son's question is not just a query about a particular event; it represents humanity's eternal quest to understand the divine grace toward sinners.

Remember, a fattened calf is not like any other calf and is not an everyday event. The servant didn't say, "Your father has killed one of the fattened calves," but "THE fattened calf." It was especially reared and fed as a centerpiece of a grand celebration, symbolizing the joyous occasion's magnitude. The decision to kill the fattened calf implies an event of the same magnitude as a wedding, a festivity involving both the family and the larger community.

The servant's words convey two main pieces of information: the younger son's return and the father's response. The manner in which the servant communicates this – noting that the son is back "safe and sound" – is significant. These words imply relief and underscore the father's primary concern: not the lost wealth or the son's rebellious actions, but the son's well-being. Notice the servant didn't say, "Your father has killed the fattened calf because your brother finally confessed his sins and repented," but because "*he has him back safe and sound.*" Repentance is important, but it wasn't what the father was after. He simply wanted to know his son was well and preferably by him once again. He wanted his heart.

While the verse doesn't directly describe the elder brother, the information he receives is poised to ignite a whirlwind of feelings. Knowing the cultural significance of the fattened calf's slaughter, he instantly grasps the magnitude of the celebration. Having remained loyal and steadfast, the older son may feel overshadowed, overlooked, and possibly undervalued. The joy over finding out a sinner is not dead but alive and well, one who squandered his inheritance, juxtaposed with the grand gesture of slaughtering the fattened calf, might feel like a slight to the older son, a challenge to his years of unwavering duty and loyalty.

Years ago, while sitting at a dinner table with some friends, one of them said, "I don't understand why we are forced, through taxation, to support the poor and needy. I worked very hard for what I have, and their fault and decisions have led them to where they are today. Their sins shouldn't be my problem." These are probably the same kind of individualistic-legalistic thoughts the older son had in his mind.

Though the father is not directly speaking in this verse, his actions speak volumes. The decision to kill the fattened calf, even before the older son's return, suggests that the father's love and joy are uncontrollable and are not contingent on the approval of anyone. His priority is the restoration of a relationship through forgiveness. The gesture transcends cultural and theological expectations and speaks of a love that values relationship over ritual and restoration over retribution.

The father's reaction, as the servant conveys, offers a compelling portrait of God's grace. The father doesn't wait for the community's consensus or even the older son's approval; he acts out of profound joy and relief. This reflects the biblical assertion that there's rejoicing in heaven when a sinner changes and repents (Luke 15:7). In the Bible, the term "repentance" is often misconstrued due to modern connotations that imply guilt or shame. However, at its core, the biblical concept of repentance, derived from the Greek word "metanoia," actually means "change of mind." For instance, when a thief stops stealing and finds a decent job instead, it means he repented; he changed his mind and ways. This change of mind prompts a shift in understanding perspective, aligning closer to God's will. Thus, repentance is about transforming one's mindset to live a more virtuous life.

In many ways, the father in this parable defies the cultural and even religious norms not only of his day but of ours as well. By all accounts, the prodigal son does not "deserve" a celebration. Yet, the father's love is not about merit but about mercy. God's love is not transactional but transformational. It's not about what we do to earn or maintain God's salvation but about God's salvation maintaining us.

'THE OLDER BROTHER BECAME ANGRY AND REFUSED TO GO IN. SO HIS FATHER WENT OUT AND PLEADED WITH HIM.'

(VERSE 28)

In his imminent reaction, the elder brother represents those who grapple with a merit-based understanding of God's love, aka "legalists." His potential feelings of injustice, confusion, and overshadowed loyalty resonate with anyone who has ever felt that their consistent efforts went unnoticed while spontaneous acts were celebrated. Interestingly, the father treated both sons equally. Both sinned against him, and his reaction was to take the initiative to mend both relationships. How amazing is the Father's grace!

I am sure some who suffered harsh legalism would love to have been able to amend this verse, perhaps to something along the lines of:

"The older brother became angry and refused to go in. So his father took out his belt, whipped him, and had the servants escort him to his room, where he continued to kick and scream."

Such a father might align with how some envision a hyper-conservative, legalistic father from the 21st century. In the cases of both the older and younger sons, the father had ample reason to chastise his children. It would be hard to fault anyone for reacting this way, especially given the public shaming not only of the younger son but also of the older son, who is throwing a tantrum in front of all the guests.

You see, in Judaism, the act of shaming someone is considered as serious as, if not worse than, murder.[1] This comparison is rooted in the metaphor that when a person is shamed, they turn so pale that it appears as if all their blood has been drained away, akin to death. It's suggested that shaming might even be worse than murder because, unlike the deceased, an individual who has been publicly shamed must endure the consequences—gossip, hatred, and humiliation—for the rest of their life.

However, and with much irony, the self-righteous legalist who gets upset with sinners in this parable is not the father but the goody-two-shoes older brother. He demonstrates that one can be involved in the Father's affairs—say as a missionary, manage His estate—say as a pastor, or represent the Father to the world—say as a Bible teacher, all without truly knowing the Father's heart. The older son was extremely involved with the father yet couldn't even fathom the thing most centered on his father's heart—loving grace:

> Bible-believing religious people often miss the gospel.
> Just because you believe in the Bible doesn't mean
> you understand it. Over and over the tax collectors,
> prostitutes, and the amoral come to Jesus, while the

---

1. See: Sefer Ha-Mitzvos, lo ta'aseh 303.

religious miss who he is.[2]

Think about how harmful religious pride can be. The story begins
with one son getting lost and ends with another, as the older son leaves
the house and refuses to re-enter. Both sons were lost. One was lost by
being very bad, while the other was lost by being self-righteously good.
Perhaps the only way for the older son to be "born again," so to speak,
is to undergo the experience his younger, no-longer-prodigal brother
already had. He likely needs to embark on his own sobering journey
of faith to help crush his religious pride.

Perhaps only when his ego is shattered will he be able to truly comprehend the Kingdom of God and step back into his father's house.
While the father clearly loves him as well, Jesus chose to end the story
with the older, religiously legalistic brother remaining outside and at
odds. It's not until we recognize the legalist in us that we can genuinely
learn to appreciate God's boundless grace and unconditional love for
all people- sinners and legalists included.

Like some today, the older son believed that his full and uncom-
promising obedience meant his father owed him something. We often
think that obedience and repentance are why God saves us. Yet, in this
story, it was the obedient child who, at the end of the parable, was left
outside the party. Legalism can be deceiving.

---

2. Tim Keller, Dec 11, 2018.

    https://twitter.com/timkellernyc/status/107227418486737715
    3

The older son's refusal to join the party is yet another pivotal emotional moment in the narrative of the Prodigal Son, emphasizing the stark contrast between the joyous father and the resentful elder brother. Remember, the societal structure of first-century Judea places a high premium on familial respect and the hierarchies therein. The elder son's decision to publicly shame and disgrace his father in such a manner reveals the depth of anger and hatred in his heart.

The firstborn son, traditionally, was not just the heir but also the future patriarch of the family. Everyone respected the older son because they knew how much power and authority he would soon have. His duty was to uphold the honor of the household and its traditions. Instead, he is doing the exact opposite. The public celebration, thrown by the father for the younger son, would traditionally be seen as an event where the elder brother's participation was almost mandatory. His abstention from it, therefore, was not a mere personal choice but a significant and public statement- the father is willing to break all norms and traditions for the sake of sinners. The father's celebration and acceptance of sinners is a new precedent and tradition the father set in place in his family's legacy.

Through this parable, Jesus aims to establish that same tradition and precedent in Jewish Israel.

The elder brother's anger is multifaceted. On the surface, it might seem like mere jealousy towards the younger sibling. However, digging deeper, it becomes clear that it is his father with whom he is truly angry. This complex mix of negative emotions the older son feels is both unexpected and profound. This dynamic harkens back to another pair of biblical brothers: Cain and Abel. Just as Cain's anger towards Abel was rooted in his own dissatisfaction and resentment towards God's acceptance of Abel's offering, the elder brother's animosity stems from his own insecurities and discontentment with his father's actions. Both situations underscore the depth and danger of pride-made jealousy.

Of course, there's an apparent sense of injustice. He had stayed, worked, and upheld family honor, yet no calf was killed for him. Instead, a calf is killed for the one person who did the opposite: bringing shame, pain, and financial loss to the family. But beyond the materialistic perspective, there's a deeper emotional wound. The celebration for the prodigal might have made the older son feel as if his years of loyalty meant less to the father than the younger son's mere return. The older son thinks his value is weighted by his works. He didn't understand the father loved his wicked young brother just as much and that his love meant a grand celebration, not punishment. That's the father's forgiveness, and it wasn't due to something the young son did; it was due to who he was- a beloved child of the father!

In the cultural context, the patriarch's role was not to chase after disgruntled family members or servants. They were supposed to come to him pleading, not the other way around! However, the father, breaking yet another societal norm, goes out to his older son just as he ran to his younger brother earlier. In both cases, before they even repented, The father's act was not about quickly resolving a family dispute in quiet but an expression of love, showcasing that the older son's feelings and presence matter to the father, even if it's because of things his son is simply unable to understand. We oftentimes don't understand God, so we storm out angry. But that doesn't mean He will burn us in fire if we don't get our act back together. In fact, it is the father who went out of his way to reason with his children in Jesus' parable.

Burning your immature, foolish child in the fire for refusing to recognize their stupidity and repent is something only an unequipped, evil parent would have done, not a good and loving parent. This action, juxtaposed with the grand feast inside, shows that while the father is joyous about the return of the prodigal son, he is equally concerned about the feelings and well-being of his older son.

The character of the father in this parable continues to serve as a profound reflection of God's nature. God's love is not just for the sinners but also for the self-righteous legalists who feel left out. In both cases, it's because they have yet to learn an important life lesson and don't fully understand the father's heart. The older son's feelings of being overlooked or undervalued can resonate with many who feel their constant service to God goes unnoticed. This verse reminds us that God sees, values, and reaches out to all – those who have strayed and those who have stayed.

God, represented by the father, doesn't dismiss the older son's feelings or chastise him for his resentment. Instead, God acknowledges those feelings, giving them space and addressing them directly. It's a portrayal of a God who is deeply relational, one who engages with our emotions, our logic, our doubts, and our frustrations. God is not the parent who screams at his child, *"How dare you question me!? How dare you speak to me this way?!"* Instead, God is able to contain all of our emotions, negative or positive, as well as our wrong beliefs about Him. These do not threaten Him nor cause Him to hate us.

The father's act of reaching out to the older son, much like his embrace of the prodigal, serves as a testament to a love that knows no limits and engages with us in our most profound moments of doubt, ensuring that we never feel left out. It is okay to be frustrated with God at times. He is big enough to contain us-all of us-including our misconceptions.

'BUT HE ANSWERED HIS FATHER, "LOOK! ALL THESE YEARS I'VE BEEN SLAVING FOR YOU AND NEVER DISOBEYED YOUR ORDERS. YET YOU NEVER GAVE ME EVEN A YOUNG GOAT SO I COULD CELEBRATE WITH MY FRIENDS."'

(VERSE 29)

Not "Father," not "Sir," but *Look!* The older son was clearly upset enough to humiliate his father out in the open. But it's also not too difficult to empathize with the older son in the story. According to the older son, his father elevated the prodigal son to a status not just equal to, but even surpassing, his own. The lavish welcome given to the prodigal son makes the older son reflect on his own years of faithful service. He resents the lack of recognition from his father, not for his material generosity but for his emotional affirmation. The older son doesn't necessarily desire a goat (suggesting that the father is not stingy); what he craves is acknowledgment.

In ancient Jewish society, the family was a microcosm of societal norms, hierarchies, and values. By now, you already know that the older son traditionally held a unique position, being the primary heir and custodian of the family's legacy. The father's decision to allocate part of the inheritance to the younger son and subsequently to host a grand celebration upon his return would've certainly upset the established norms. The older son's reference to never having received a young goat indicates an absence of public recognition of his loyalty and obedience. But here, we also see the true legalistic heart of the son, who believes his father enslaved him.

There's a profound depth of emotion in the older son's words. *"All these years I've been slaving for you"* conveys more than just loyalty; it hints at a relationship that felt more obligatory than affectionate. His use of the term "slaving" shows a perception of servitude rather than sonship, duty rather than delight, and legalistic fear rather than grace. This sense of servitude is compounded by his assertion of his own righteousness: *"I never disobeyed your orders."* Evidently, he viewed life in black and white, good and evil, and exclusivity. He views his relationship with his father as more transactional than relational. It's about what he does, not who he is. That's how many of the Pharisees and Scribes viewed God and how some Christians see him today.

Religion is often motivated by fear, operating under the belief that fear of punishment leads to repentance. However, Jesus taught that it is God's grace and kindness that lead to genuine repentance. Fear doesn't transform the heart; it merely erects barriers around it. In contrast, love truly changes the heart, resulting in a transformation of character. The Bible describes God as love (1 John 4:8), not as fear,[1] and "there is no fear in love" (1 John 4:18). The gospel is not about

---

1. I invite you to explore the meaning of the Hebrew word "fear" (such as in "The fear of the Lord is the beginning of knowledge;" Proverbs 1:7), as well as other Hebrew words that often get mistranslated in my book, "Lost in Translation: 15 Hebrew Words to Transform Your Christian Faith."

what we do to earn or maintain His love (that's what the religious leaders believed) but about God's love maintaining us!

The core of the elder son's distress is revealed in the latter part of the verse. It isn't so much about what his prodigal brother was given by their father, but rather what the father had never granted him: public recognition. His underlying motivation was rooted in self-interest. Notably, the elder son spoke not of celebrating with his father or family but of rejoicing with his friends. His complaint is steeped in entitlement. He believes he earned his father's love. In this light, he is not so different from his younger brother; both are primarily concerned with their own desires.

The elder brother struggled with the notion that his father could lovingly embrace and bless perceived wrongdoers; he yearned to see "justice" enacted! The father grasped a truth that eluded his elder son. His children, though loved, are imperfect; they are bound by their human limitations and fallibilities. They're still navigating life's labyrinth, and their missteps or unlearned lessons don't diminish their father's love or incite his wrath. This insight is equally pertinent to us: we're all journeying, endeavoring to understand life, ourselves, and the Divine. While some of us might navigate it more adeptly than others, and a few may even lose their way, God's love remains unwavering. His embrace extends to both the self-righteous and the seemingly lost.

While the verse doesn't directly elaborate on the father's immediate response, the fact that the older son feels comfortable voicing his resentment indicates a level of transparency in their relationship. The father never enforced his respect on anyone, as evidenced by how his son allows himself to speak to him. However, that's because the father wants his sons' respect to be based on love, not fear. It's a testament to the father's character, making him approachable even in moments of disagreement.

This verse mirrors many who might feel like the older son in their relationship with God. It addresses the sentiments of those who've been consistently righteous, obeying commandments, and yet feeling like their loyalty goes unnoticed, especially when juxtaposed against God's abundant grace towards those who err.

Moreover, the older son is just as much "a sinner" in the eyes of his father, much like his younger brother, because his sentiment echoes feelings of pride and entitlement, which we know God hates (Proverbs 11:2; James 4:6). This perspective often creeps into religion. There's a subtle message here: Being in God's house doing God's ministry and good deeds doesn't necessarily mean one knows God's heart. In fact, few do. It's possible to be physically close, with all the right seminary titles and degrees, yet emotionally and spiritually distant.

The older son's grievances pose a pivotal theological question: Is God's love and reward transactional, dependent on our actions, or is it inherent and unconditional? The son's attitude illuminates how religion frequently frames our relationship with God in terms of merit. It often interprets blessings as rewards and hardships as retributions. But this is not how we should view God. When we encounter sin, we experience pain and suffering. At times, that anguish prompts us to inflict hurt upon others. When they get hurt, they continue to hurt others as well in a vicious, never-ending cycle. The notion that we are all interconnected and bear responsibility for one another contradicts modern hyper-individualistic beliefs and is a truth God consistently endeavored to instill in Israel.[2]

This is a gentle reminder of something we should all know, yet we rarely understand the depth of what it means: Our deeds and works are crucial because we can't love one another unless we are good to one another. However, God's love is not performance-based. Like the father in the parable, sin doesn't diminish God's grace. In fact, "where sin increased, grace abounded all the more" (Romans 5:20). God's love is always willing to feast with both sinners and the self-righteous equally. We just need to align ourselves with what it means.

---

2. For example: Exodus 32; Numbers 14; Numbers 16; Numbers 25; Joshua 7; 2 Samuel 24 and 1 Chronicles 21; 1 Samuel 15.

"But when this son of yours who has squandered your property with prostitutes comes home, you kill the fattened calf for him!"

(Verse 30)

T he older son continues to express his frustration, hurt, and jealousy over the celebratory response his father has towards the return of the prodigal younger son.

In the ancient Jewish cultural setting, the return of a lost family member would undoubtedly be a cause for joy. Yet, not in the case of this family. By saying, *"This son of yours,"* he distances himself from his brother, almost disowning him. The elder brother's years of loyalty, obedience, and hard work seem to him to go unrewarded, making the celebration for the wayward brother feel like a slap in the face.

Understanding the societal implications of the younger son's actions is essential. He not only asked for his inheritance prematurely, which in itself was a significant affront, but he also squandered it in "wild living," which the older son explicitly identifies as spending on prostitutes. The mentioning of prostitutes is not at all accidental and we may also safely assume that prostitutes stood in the crowd, listening to Jesus' parable.

In the Gospel of Luke, when Jesus mentions prostitutes, He's doing more than just referring to a marginalized group; He's tapping into a rich tapestry of stories from Israel's history. For instance, Rahab, a prostitute from Jericho, expresses faith in God and saves the spies, Israel, and her family. She is later heralded in the genealogy of Jesus (Matthew 1:5). Similarly, Tamar, who posed as a prostitute, through her bold faith, ensured the continuation of Judah's lineage, ultimately leading to the birth of King David. Tamar was also mentioned in the genealogy of Jesus (Matthew 1:3).

So, when the Pharisees and religious elites of Jesus' day scorned and shunned prostitutes, they missed the broader biblical narrative of redemption, grace, and unexpected mercy. Jesus' inclusive approach starkly contrasted with the legalistic view, highlighting a God who doesn't just tolerate the marginalized and sinners but actively uses them in His kingdom.

From the perspective of the religious leaders, associating with prostitutes was deeply taboo, casting shame not only on the individual but on their entire family. Thus, the elder son's mention of prostitutes was more than just a pointed jab at his brother; it underscored the depth of shame he felt his younger brother had inflicted on their family. This mirrors the sentiment of the religious leaders in Jesus' time, who frequently criticized Him for his interactions with women, some of whom were likely prostitutes:

> "If this man were a prophet, he would know who is touching him and what kind of woman she is—that she is a sinner." (Luke 7:39)

This was a challenge to Jesus' prophetic legitimacy. How could a true prophet of God allow a prostitute to touch him? This sentiment is rooted in the religious understanding that holiness requires separation from sin and sinners.[1]

However, Jesus counters this mindset throughout his ministry. By incorporating sinners such as prostitutes throughout his gospel, Luke highlights God's universal love, grace, and the upside-down nature of the Kingdom of God, where those seen as "last" and "least" in society can be the first in the Kingdom. More specifically, Jesus underscores the point that God's grace is available to everyone, including those who religious leaders and their society have shunned.

Therefore, it becomes clear that Jesus is making a deliberate point. He is challenging the Pharisees' and other religious leaders' self-righteousness, narrow understanding of holiness, and misplaced confidence in their own status. He emphasizes that God's love and grace extend far beyond the boundaries they have constructed and that faith, rather than societal status or perceived righteousness, is what transforms people's lives and, therefore, what matters the most in the

---

1. In biblical times, kings were anointed by men. Yet, in a beautiful twist, Jesus, the King of kings, was anointed not by the influential men of his time but by women, a prostitute included (Luke 7:36-50; Matthew 26:6-13). This is a powerful reminder of how Jesus upends societal norms, valuing the heartfelt actions of the marginalized and overlooked. It underscores that in God's kingdom, it's not status or gender that matters but genuine faith and love. It's a message of hope: everyone can have a role in the Kingdom of God, no matter their background.

Kingdom of God.[2]

The older brother leveled the same accusation at his sibling that religious legalists often hurled at sinners — squandering resources on immoral pursuits like prostitution. Yet, in the parable, the father remained unfazed. After all, it was his resources that the son had lost, not the brother. Besides, the son's missteps were no grounds for disdain or rejection and certainly not an excuse to hate or cancel his sinful son.

A moment of reflection is sparked when we consider Jesus' words: *"Truly I tell you, the tax collectors and the prostitutes are entering the kingdom of God ahead of you"* (Matthew 21:31). How dare we exclude those whom Jesus openly welcomed? This isn't a dismissal of righteousness but rather a condemnation of self-righteousness. The Parable of the Prodigal Son drives this point home: while sins are undoubtedly harmful, it's our self-righteousness and pride that often stretch the gap between us and God. From Pharisees to monarchs, the Bible chronicles those who were blinded by pride, leading them astray.

Ironically, it was the religious purists whom Christ publicly condemned (Matthew 23) and who led the charge in rejecting and crucifying Him. Meanwhile, in Luke 7:37-38, a prostitute employed a costly perfume—traditionally used for seduction—to anoint Jesus. This poignant gesture transformed a symbol of sin into an emblem of faith. Just as the perfume was repurposed, so too can our past mistakes be redeemed by God's grace.

The older brother brings up the celebratory meal for the second

---

2. In my book, 'The "Gospel" of Divine Abuse,' I delve deeper into the subjects of sin, faith, and righteousness, examining them from a Jewish-roots perspective.

time. Despite having the means to host his own celebration, he chose not to. Who was holding him back? The younger brother certainly wasn't in a position to host such a feast. If the older brother's intentions were loving, he could have offered to help with the expenses, showcasing his love and appreciation for both his father and sibling. Instead, his bitterness becomes evident. It seems he hoped for his younger brother to face punishment and humiliation and be treated as a sinful adversary. However, the father never viewed the prodigal son as an enemy but as his cherished child.

Let's reflect: In a similar situation, how would our hearts react? Would we mirror the older brother, holding onto self-righteous anger and distancing ourselves from those who wronged us? Or, could we channel the father's spirit, braving societal judgment, family tensions, and personal pain all in the name of love? Faced with a chance to rejoice when those who hurt us are found alive and reconciled, would we join the celebration or stand aloof, consumed by resentment? This festive gathering is more than a son's homecoming; it symbolizes the profound power of forgiveness and restoration.

While the verse doesn't directly address the prodigal son's feelings at this moment, one can imagine that having just returned from a place of deep despair, hearing such accusations—especially during a celebration in his honor—must have felt like salt being poured on fresh wounds. This situation parallels that of some Christians who, instead of protecting a sinner's honor as Joseph did when he thought Mary had committed adultery and chose to divorce her in secret, opt to gossip and loudly proclaim the sinner's faults in an attempt to humiliate, ridicule, shame, and cancel them.

In many ways, the older son represents the legalistic approach to religion — the belief that salvation is to be earned and kept by good deeds, loyalty, and unwavering dedication. His resentment stems from the perception that he's been righteous and done everything by the book, yet the return home of a sinner his father chooses to celebrate reveals his true colors.

A legalist could be defined as someone who fails to understand that God's salvation is purely by grace—the very grace they are supposed to extend to others in return. Genuine faith isn't, "My faith gives me the right to judge others." Instead, it should prompt us to ask difficult questions about ourselves and drive us toward self-improvement and producing the fruits of the spirit. Fortunately for the legalistic older son, the father also went outside to pursue him. God loves both sinners and legalists alike.

We often witness people who become gracious, compassionate, and loving individuals due to their past failures. These experiences taught them life lessons such as empathy, compassion, and humility. In contrast, those who have always considered themselves "perfect" frequently become prideful and self-righteous, much like the older brother in the parable.

The father's actions reflect God's nature — boundless, forgiving, and celebratory at the return of the lost. It underscores the idea that God's love isn't something to be earned but freely given, especially to those who need it the most. The killing of the fattened calf is a symbolic reminder, not of a father pouring his wrath in anger, but of the great lengths God goes to show His love and celebrate it.

The gospel of Jesus is not merely a reminder that we are sinners—we all, believers and non-believers alike, have a conscience and should already be well aware of our imperfect and limited nature.

Rather, the gospel serves as a testament that God loves us despite our imperfections. His love is what gives us the power for transformation. God's ways are not our own. While humans operate mainly in a realm of transactions, merits, and rewards, God operates mainly in a realm of grace, love, and forgiveness. It emphasizes that no one is beyond redemption and that everyone can partake in the divine feast if only they wish to, no matter their past. God always wants to party with us; it is we who often don't.

"MY SON," THE FATHER SAID, "YOU ARE ALWAYS WITH ME, AND EVERYTHING I HAVE IS YOURS. BUT WE HAD TO CELEBRATE AND BE GLAD, BECAUSE THIS BROTHER OF YOURS WAS DEAD AND IS ALIVE AGAIN; HE WAS LOST AND IS FOUND."

(VERSES 31–32)

Consider the contrast between the older brother's distant phrase, *"This son of yours,"* and the father's intimate response, *"My son."* The father refrains from saying *"you idiot"*—even though one could argue that the older son (well, both sons) acted foolishly—choosing instead to call him *"my son."* The older son's rebellious state of disobedience doesn't alter his father's love for him. Similarly, in the spiritual realm, we remain God's children even at times when we disobey Him. However, if we persist in our stubbornness and disobedience, we may miss out on the celebration and rewards. The same is true for the prodigal son; his father's love for him never wavered, but he did lose his inheritance and years of his life. Our sins have consequences; sin always comes at a cost. Yet, even when we drift far away from God and find ourselves eating pigs' food, His love doesn't change. In fact, it is often through these kinds of journeys that we come to *"grasp how wide and long and high and deep"* God's love is (Ephesians 3:18).

Importantly, the father never exclaims, *"Ha! See! This behavior proves you were never truly my child!"* Neither does the father say, *"You are being disobedient and disrespectful! This is it! You are no longer my son!"* The older son's pride, sins, and shaming of his father, much like his younger brother's case, do nothing to change the father's love. This scenario brings to mind Paul's plea to the pagans at the Areopagus, where he says, *"For in Him we live and move and exist, as even some of your own poets have said, 'For we also are His children.'"* (Acts 17:28). In the same way, the father loves those who recognize him, those who don't, and those who think they do but actually don't yet fully do—as his beloved children whom he loves.

The older son's previous grievances, expressed in verse 30, arise from a place of perceived injustice. After years of loyalty and hard work, he felt overshadowed by the wayward brother's return. In his heart, there's a battle between the duty he's performed and the recognition he feels he deserves. The father's words in this verse are directed precisely at these feelings. When the father says, *"You are always with me,"* he's acknowledging the older son's constant presence, commitment, and sacrifices. The affirmation that *"everything I have is yours"* serves as a reminder of his birthright and the fact that, in essence, by giving the younger son his portion earlier, everything remaining indeed belongs to the older son now.

In addressing both of his sons, the father did not rebuke them by choosing words of condemnation. There was no criticism or disappointment but a comforting assurance of his unconditional love.

While he could have scolded both sons, the young son for his reckless actions that brought shame on the family and the older son for his self-righteousness, pride, and disobedience, he instead focused on imparting a sense of acceptance and belonging to each of them. He recognizes and addresses the older son's pain with compassion and understanding while simultaneously celebrating the return of his young son. His language served as a verbal embrace, enveloping them in a sense of security and love and reminding them that they were both cherished family members despite their flaws and shortcomings. If the father mirrors our Father in heaven, then this parable sets a high standard for loving those who hurt us.

Just as the father in the parable acknowledges the older son's pain, so too does God understand our struggles. Many on their spiritual journey might identify with the older son. They've walked loyally with God, yet sometimes feel He blesses others—even those who have wronged them—more generously. This can birth feelings of jealousy and resentment. Such sentiments often give rise to judgment and legalism, a reflection of the older brother's attitude and, unfortunately, a trait evident in some Christians today.

The affirmation, *"everything I have is yours,"* also invites reflection on the nature of divine blessings. Often, humans measure blessings only in tangible terms – wealth, success, and health. But God's blessings also encompass peace, joy, and kindness (Galatians 5:22-23). We can relish not just God's material blessings, which are undeniably generous, but even more so, His presence, which is incomparable. Much like the older son who failed to see the vast treasures at his fingertips, we, too, can occasionally miss out on recognizing the immense blessings already surrounding us.

Furthermore, this verse emphasizes the theme of religious jealousy. The older son's grievances arose from a place of envy towards the prodigal son. This mirrors how humans sometimes view others' blessings with envy rather than joy. The father's reassurance serves as a reminder that God has enough love and grace for everyone, and His blessings for one do not diminish what He has in store for another. After all, God owns *"the cattle on a thousand hills"* (Psalm 50:10).

While celebrations might be thrown for those who were lost and are found, those who never strayed are never taken for granted. God's love doesn't compare or measure; it simply gives – generously and ceaselessly.

"But we had to celebrate and be glad because this brother of yours was dead and is alive again; he was lost and is found."

In *"we had to,"* the father implies, *"we couldn't wait."* While some celebrations, like weddings, are meticulously planned and have set dates, others emerge spontaneously. This spontaneity is crucial because it captures the essence of genuine emotion and uncontainable joy. The father's impromptu feast demonstrates the urgency and depth of his love; he couldn't wait for a scheduled moment to express his relief and happiness. It emphasizes the idea that true love and redemption don't adhere to human schedules or conventions but are powerful, immediate reactions of the heart.

In the prevailing Jewish perspective of the time, there existed a strong belief in God as a just and righteous judge. He couldn't simply overlook sin without meting out some form of penalty. Against this backdrop, the idea of someone committing a grave mistake and yet being received without punishment—instead celebrated upon return—would have undoubtedly jarred many listeners. Squandering one's inheritance wasn't just a personal failure; it tarnished the family's reputation. After all, society often gauges parents based on their children's behavior; wayward children cast a shadow over their upbringing. So, in such a context, it's understandable why many would expect the prodigal son to be met with disdain and ostracism rather than a hearty welcome.

Some posit that before forgiving someone, there's a need to exact punishment on the wrongdoer. But there's a distinction between punishment and forgiveness. Punishment places the burden on the offender, while forgiveness shifts that burden to the one granting pardon. Consider a scenario: we have a disagreement, and I upset you. If you decide to forgive, it's you who bears the emotional brunt, while I benefit from your forgiveness. Now, imagine a different situation where you damage something of mine; I could either retaliate by damaging your property or demand compensation—both options would mean you bear the cost. However, if I choose forgiveness, I'm essentially shouldering that loss while you walk away unburdened.

In the parable of the prodigal son, the act of forgiving costs the father not only a substantial part of his fortune but also emotional anguish. If the father represents God in this story, then the notion held by some contemporary Christians—that God needed to inflict pain, abuse, and torture Jesus to grant us forgiveness—seems misplaced.[1] God didn't turn to violence as a path to forgiveness; He took on the cost Himself to provide it.

---

1. I discuss this topic extensively in my book, 'The "Gospel" of Divine Abuse: Redeeming the Gospel from Gruesome Popular Preaching of an Abusive and Violent God.'

The father's words in this verse resonate with joy, relief, and celebration. He is concerned not about the lost wealth but about his lost son. His reference to the son as "dead" and "alive again" speaks of a dead relationship that has now been resurrected. This choice of words also implies the deep pain and feelings of grief the father must have felt during his son's absence, considering him as good as dead. His joy at the return is a joy of resurrection—of life where there were once only memories. It wasn't that the father would send a delegation to find, capture, and stone him to death if he failed to return; it's that his son would continue to be lost and "die in his sin."

The father's remark, *"This brother of yours,"* might carry a touch of gentle sarcasm or perhaps a hint of humor, aiming to lighten the mood. Yet, it also underscores the elder son's bond with the prodigal, highlighting their kinship and shared roots. It isn't just any festivity; it's for "your brother." Similarly, we sometimes overlook that the very sinners we might disdain are also God's creation. Rather than preaching that sinners should flee from God in fear, we should convey that God actually longs to embrace them, emphasizing His love and invitation.

God's perspective, as voiced by the father, doesn't dwell on past mistakes. Instead, it focuses on growth. The father's joy is unburdened by societal expectations or the weight of past errors. This mirrors God's approach to repentant sinners, wherein He doesn't hold onto past sins but embraces the returning individual with open arms- each and every time. Even if the prodigal son would leave again tomorrow, his father would eagerly await him again. Likewise, God's forgiveness is without limits. Since that is true about God, it should also be true about us – Christians should always extend forgiveness. Not once, not twice, but always:

> Then Peter came to Jesus and asked, "Lord, how many times shall I forgive my brother or sister who sins against me? Up to seven times?" Jesus answered, "I tell you, not seven times, but seventy-seven times. (Matthew 18:21-22)

Being "lost" isn't just about distance from God; it's about navigating through solitude and enduring life's struggles seemingly alone. But, when we're "found," it signifies more than just closeness; it's a communion, a union with Him. The jubilant celebration of the father in the parable isn't just a random act of joy; it's a manifestation of how deeply God longs for every one of His children to find their way back to Him. The beauty of it? No matter how lost, how astray, or how deep in despair you might feel, there's always a path leading back to the embrace of our loving Father. This sentiment stands at the very core of the Gospel. It's the embodiment of God's unending, jubilant love, ever-ready to welcome and cherish anyone who turns His way. It underscores the unparalleled value God places on each soul, irrespective of their past deeds. So remember, no matter how far you think you've drifted or the mistakes you've made, your return is always met with divine rejoicing. The culmination of this parable offers us Jesus' profound message: hope, redemption, and the unfathomable, all-encompassing love of the Heavenly Father await everyone.

AFTERWORD

Many who have left a mark on the world—philanthropists, teachers, inventors, entrepreneurs, and artists—often remind us that failure is an inevitable step toward growth and maturity. Sometimes, the failure is our fault; other times, it is not. Their journeys tell us that imperfection isn't a dead end but rather a necessary bridge to advancement. Likewise, in the spiritual realm, our learning path, marked by stumbles and recoveries, is essential for spiritual growth, maturation, and self-realization.

Consider this: God created us emotional beings because feelings serve as powerful teachers. Yet, the depth of our emotions often relies on our experiences. From the depths of agony, sorrow, frustration, loss, despair, and grief, we encounter the negative effects of sin within and around us. Experiencing these emotions not only deepens our understanding of sin's impact but also introduces us to concepts of forgiveness, grace, empathy, and compassion. In essence, it's often through our failures and pain that we come to truly understand and appreciate the nature of love. For instance, King David's transgressions gave rise to the poetic Psalms that praise God for His forgiveness and grace. Such testimonies emphasize that firsthand experience surpasses mere theoretical knowledge. David could fully understand the depth of God's forgiveness only because he felt the burden of transgression and the subsequent relief of redemption.

In His boundless wisdom, God could have predetermined salvation or saved us without the challenges of this world or even the need to create it. However, He opted for a journey that immerses us in experiences—revealing His nature, grace, love, and compassion. This pilgrimage is invaluable. Thus, let us embrace every stumble and setback, for they serve as compass points, directing us toward a richer comprehension of ourselves, the world, and God's divine nature. This is also why the Bible is a narrative full of stories, not merely a manual or textbook.

The Bible is filled with stories of how God uses the greatest of sinners to provide redemption to their people. Moses, Rahab, David, and Paul—individuals who, by societal standards, were flawed, yet they were chosen to be used by God to shine in His kingdom. This highlights a central biblical theme: God often chooses the outcasts, the sinners, and those spurned by society. It's a clarion call for us not just to hope for everyone—no matter how far they run from God— but to work for their inclusion and redemption actively.

Jesus employed the Parable of the Prodigal Son to challenge the strict, legalistic religious sentiments of His time. He consistently reached out to those marginalized as "sinners," unsettling the religious elite. Through this parable, He beckons everyone to witness the transformative power of God's love, highlighting that those who are keenly aware of their flaws and brokenness are especially primed to embrace God's infinite grace and be used by Him in His kingdom.

"Life is in the blood," as stated in Leviticus 17:11. Those who are perfect inherently possess eternal life, so Christ's sacrifice wasn't for their benefit but for sinners. One sacrifices one's own life only for those one deeply loves, not for those one detests. Christ's sacrificial act stands as irrefutable evidence of God's profound love for sinners, not His disdain.

In our current era of "great exodus" from churches and "faith deconstruction," churches and their members must reflect on this parable's significance. Do we prioritize our image and religious pride over genuine compassion? Do we embrace the outcasts and sinners as Jesus did or further push them away from God?

In our individual and mutual journey of faith, let us continually draw lessons when we fail, embrace growth, demonstrate God's grace, and love relentlessly, understanding that every stumble is an opportunity for spiritual formation and a chance to draw closer to the Father. The sins and demons you face are not necessarily the same as others face, so don't judge them for having different struggles than you do. Instead, lift, encourage, and serve others, even if you feel they are your enemies. Easier said than done, I know, but that's what the gospel is all about- we've been forgiven so that we may forgive others, too.

My heartfelt encouragement for sinners (myself included) is this: Rise, stand tall, and keep moving forward. Remember, you are profoundly loved by God!

To the legalists (myself included), my earnest plea: Extend grace to sinners. They likely had a more challenging life and are at a different stage in their journey than you are, but every stage is a step closer to understanding God's boundless love and grace. Let's support and uplift each other, recognizing that everyone's path is unique, but our destination in God's love is the same!

***

If you have not yet experienced the love of God, and I'm not speaking of religious practices, I invite you to give God a chance. God is not fear; He is love (1 John 4:16). If you happen to be Jewish and have reservations, I invite you to contact me through my website.[1] I also have several books that might help you make a well-informed decision!

To the rest of you: If this short book has been a blessing to you, please consider leaving a review. Nothing warms an author's heart more than receiving a thoughtful rating and review. It doesn't have to be long and would bless me greatly!!

P.S. I would appreciate your prayers as I'm seeking new ministry opportunities. I also invite you to check out my several other books on my Amazon page!

Thank you, and Shalom!

Eitan Bar

---

1. www.eitan.bar

Made in the USA
Middletown, DE
16 July 2025

10744465R00071